Clean Eating for Beginners

*Falafel Baby Green Salad,
page 67*

CLEAN EATING

for Beginners

75 RECIPES AND 21-DAY MEAL PLAN
FOR HEALTHY LIVING

Isadora Baum

Photography by Marija Vidal

ROCKRIDGE
PRESS

Interior and Cover Designer: Jennifer Hsu
Art Producer: Sue Bischofberger
Editor: Kelly Koester
Production Manager: Jose Olivera
Production Editor: Melissa Edeburn

Photography © 2021 Marija Vidal. Food styling by Victoria Woollard.

Paperback ISBN: 978-1-64876-459-2
eBook ISBN: 978-1-64876-460-8

R0

To those embracing a clean eating lifestyle, as well as those just beginning, eager to create their own magic and ignite that inner spark. With a turn of the page, there's a lifetime of change.

CONTENTS

INTRODUCTION

The types of food you eat really do affect the way your mind and body function. With a little practice, you can train your palate to truly crave and enjoy foods that are clean, unprocessed, and nutrient dense—foods that will improve your cognition and give your body both immediate and sustainable energy. These foods also have mood-boosting benefits, so routinely consuming them will enhance your emotional well-being and quality of life.

A lot of information about health and dieting is available, but learning which foods are healthy and which should be avoided can be daunting. That's where I come in! I have coached many clients along their journeys to cleaner eating, and I am here to help you, too.

This book will teach you the principles of clean eating, which involves cooking with whole, unprocessed produce, lean meats, plant proteins, fish, and whole grains. Along with information about how to bring these foods into your life, you'll find a 21-day starter meal plan that utilizes recipes in the book. The recipes are easy to make for weeknight meals, have minimal ingredient lists (some use five or fewer ingredients), and offer ingredient swaps and meal prepping tips.

This book will help you get the hang of clean eating quickly. The best part? You'll save the big bucks: Meal prepping can help you budget wisely and cut back on waste, so you really get your money's worth.

Excited? Let's get started.

Part One

WELCOME TO CLEAN EATING

Chapter One

STARTING FRESH

We all know the phrase, "You are what you eat," and there is some truth to it because what you eat on a daily basis influences your health—for better or worse.

If you've turned to clean eating, you will notice the perks, for both short- and long-term health. As it becomes routine, this new wholesome lifestyle will affect your day-to-day well-being, so you can feel *good* about what you're putting in your mouth and be more productive in whatever you set your mind and body to achieve.

What Does It Mean to Eat Clean?

Let's be real: "Dieting" doesn't sound fun. It often feels restrictive and solely weight-loss focused, rather than a means to living a healthy, balanced lifestyle, one that includes a diet rich in wholesome, nutritious foods that will fuel your body and boost your mood.

That's where "clean eating" comes in, a term that's risen in popularity due to its simple, easy approach and flexibility, as the goal is to fill your plate with fresh, naturally sourced whole foods and minimize the intake of processed foods. Though they can be tasty, processed foods are typically high in sodium, sugar, carbs, and calories, as they tend to use nonhealthy cooking oils, and may include additives that can put our bodies' health at risk.

Clean eating encourages cooking at home and dedicating time to meal prep—the latter being a great tool for simplifying mealtimes, cutting down on food waste, and better budgeting—and it means no foods are "off limits," as they are in other types of diets.

With clean eating, you can ditch that processed bag of chips and bake your own apple or sweet potato chips at home! Craving a candy bar? You can still satisfy that sugar fix, but with homemade Chocolate-Coconut Protein Truffles (page 55) or Chocolate-Drizzled Almond Rice Squares (page 112), instead. Rather than a structured diet full of restrictions, the clean eating approach is a shift in thinking about what you eat. And while you're minimizing, you're not saying good-bye forever! It's just a matter of making the majority of the diet about nonprocessed foods—that's not so scary, right?

BENEFITS WORTH CELEBRATING

Beyond the mere pleasure of a flavorful and filling meal, there are several benefits to eating clean. Here are a few to note:

1. **Improves your immune system**. You're eating nutritionally dense foods and getting an array of essential vitamins and minerals needed for a healthy immune system.

2. **Increases athletic performance**. Consuming a good mix of protein, fats, and fiber-packed carbs will fuel you to perform your best, as well as fully recover afterward. Eating sweet, carb-laden snacks will slow you down and decrease the efficiency of your workout.

3. **Helps you snooze soundly**. By eating clean foods, you'll get more zzz's by falling asleep faster and sleeping more soundly through-out the night. Avoid chocolate, sugar, and other stimulants before bed as well!

4. **Keeps your skin young and fresh**. Fruits and veggies have anti-oxidants that fight free-radical damage caused by aging and can prevent wrinkles and acne. Plus, they hydrate the skin.

5. **Stabilizes energy levels**. Clean eating provides sustainable energy for a peppier mood to brighten your day and keep you focused.

6. **Boosts cognitive function**. Foods that are high in protein, unsaturated fats, vitamin D, and iron all support brain health to help ward off Alzheimer's and improve focus and memory retention.

7. **Promotes heart health**. A clean eating diet keeps your ticker in good shape, with reduced risk of heart disease, stroke, high blood pressure, and high cholesterol.

Five Principles of Clean Eating

Clean eating can be simple—and habitual. Here are its five main principles:

Choosing Whole Foods

Food in its raw and most natural state retains its nutrients and lacks any harmful or foreign additives. It also lacks sugars, salt, and other types of chemicals that may be found in processed foods, which means you get all the good stuff—without the junk. And you can cook whole foods any way you like for a variety of yummy, nutritious meals.

Whole foods include whole fruits and veggies, fish, poultry, and lean cuts of meat, such as beef or pork, whole grains or wheat, gluten-free grains such as oats and quinoa, as well as dairy products like unprocessed cheese or plain Greek yogurt.

Avoiding Processed Foods

Processed foods often have long ingredient lists with names you can't pronounce, let alone know what they are! When you're grocery shopping, these long ingredient lists can serve as red flags, since there's no proof that these types of additives are good for your body (nor that they don't cause harm!).

When you eat something that is overly processed, you're consuming a higher sugar, sodium, and likely calorie count than you'd get from a whole food in its most natural form. You can use fats or oils of your choosing (like heart-healthy olive or avocado oil) as well as techniques, such as roasting or grilling (instead of frying), to reduce consumption of unhealthy fats and calories. You can also cut back on refined carbohydrates by using nuts and seeds as a coating, rather than bread crumbs. And you can flavor with spices and herbs, rather than salt and syrups.

Cooking Your Own Meals

When you cook your own meals, you can put love into each dish and know it will benefit your body and health while still being satisfying and delicious. You'll know exactly what you're consuming and what's going into your body. Plus, many people find cooking to be meditative, as a way to unwind after a busy day or as a hobby, where you can hone your skills alone or with someone else.

An added perk? You can save some cash by budgeting wisely at the grocery store and meal prepping. Using the same ingredients for a variety of meals and snacks will cut down on food waste, on the dollars spent during the week (good-bye pricey lunches and snacks around the office or at the airport), and both the time and effort of whipping up a fresh meal each day.

Eating to Feel Good (and Full)

Our bodies won't feel satiated unless we fill up with the right set of nutrients, such as lean protein, healthy fats (like unsaturated and omega-3s), and complex carbs, which are high in fiber. Consuming these foods will make you feel full longer and help you avoid mindless munching and the resulting excess calories. Eating the right nutrients puts you in tune with your body—you'll be better able to understand the difference between actual hunger cues and random impulses to eat, which can throw you off course on any wellness journey.

Minimizing Salt and Sugar

Eating foods that are high in sodium can make you feel bloated, thirsty (all that salt), tired, and then hungry all over again—ironically craving *more* salty foods. Why? As you eat more salty or sweet foods, your body craves those same foods and at the same time, your appetite isn't suppressed. So, you'll stay in this cycle without recognizing satiety cues or feeling compelled to grab a healthier snack instead. By reducing salt and sugar intake, you will naturally crave foods that fall into the clean eating category. You'll better avoid weight gain and other potential health problems, which can come from a consistently high intake of these foods.

FOODS TO ENJOY, EAT IN MODERATION, AND AVOID

When thinking about what foods to eat, consider the colors of the rainbow and fill your plate with foods that cover a range of hues. Here are some foods to enjoy freely, to eat in moderation, and to avoid.

FOODS TO ENJOY

- Acai
- Avocado
- Banana
- Berries
- Bright-colored, nonstarchy veggies, such as artichokes, asparagus, beets, bell peppers, celery, cucumber, eggplant, jicama, kohlrabi, leeks, mushrooms, okra, onions, squash, sugar snap peas, tomatoes, and zucchini
- Coconut
- Cruciferous, nonstarchy veggies, such as broccoli, Brussels sprouts, cabbage, cauliflower, radish, and turnips
- Kiwi
- Leafy greens, such as arugula, bok choy, collard greens, kale, spinach, and Swiss chard
- Melon
- Papaya
- Pineapple
- Stone fruits, such as apricots, cherries, mangos, peaches, and plums

FOODS TO EAT IN MODERATION

- Beans and legumes, such as black beans, chickpeas, and edamame
- Beef, lean
- Chocolate, unsweetened dark
- Cottage cheese
- Eggs
- Fish and shellfish

- Natural sweeteners, such as dates, honey, and maple syrup
- Poultry, lean
- Soy sauce
- Starchy veggies, such as butternut squash, carrots, potatoes, sweet potatoes, taro, and yams
- Tofu
- Whole grains (including whole wheat), such as barley, brown rice, bulgur, couscous, oatmeal, quinoa, whole-grain bread, and wild rice
- Yogurt, 0% plain Greek

FOODS TO AVOID

- Added sweeteners, such as agave syrup, brown sugar, and sugar
- Artificial sweetners
- Butter and ghee
- Fried foods and fast foods
- Hydrogenated oils, such as palm oil and trans fats
- Margarine
- Processed sweets and snacks, such as candy bars and potato chips
- Soda
- Sugary coffee and sports drinks, such as fancy coffee drinks with sugar syrups and electrolyte drinks that are high in sugar

Building a Balanced Meal

A balanced meal combines the macronutrients (protein, fats, and carbs) as well as micronutrients (vitamins and minerals) needed to fuel your body and keep you full for longer. The best sources of these nutrients come from whole foods and high-quality products that are clean and minimally processed or completely unprocessed.

Every meal should include protein, good fats, high fiber, and complex carbs and an array of essential other nutrients, like iron, magnesium, potassium, B vitamins, vitamin C, vitamin D, antioxidants, and more. Whether you choose a more high-carb diet or a lower-carb one, or one that's more plant-based or one that includes lean and clean animal protein—the strategy is all about combining foods from each group. Here's a winning formula for building a balanced meal the clean eating way.

Powerful Proteins

Protein is great for keeping the metabolism up, boosting satiety and productivity, as well as recovering from muscle damage post-workout.

You can get great protein from lean animal sources and fatty fish, as well as from plants. Lean protein examples include salmon, tuna, nuts and nut butter, seeds, soy protein like edamame and tofu, whole grains like quinoa, and leafy and cruciferous greens like spinach, broccoli, and Brussels sprouts.

It's super easy to make sure you're getting enough protein with each meal. If you're cutting back on meat, pair plant options to get the protein you need. For example, combine black beans, edamame, and quinoa for a protein-packed meal.

Filling Fats

Despite what you may have heard, fats will keep you fuller longer, so don't fear them! Although fats have more calories, healthy fats also help your body function and keep cravings at bay.

Clean fats include those from unsaturated sources or omega-3s. Saturated fat, which is found in red meat and coconut oil, for example, isn't totally off-limits (these foods should be eaten in moderation), but you should make sure the bulk of your fat intake consists of unsaturated and omega-3 fats.

Sources include fatty fish like salmon or tuna, nuts and seeds, or that powerful green fruit—the mighty avocado. These foods will all help you get your fill of healthy fat. You can also find healthy fats in certain cooking oils like olive or avocado oil.

Complex Carbs

Although you want to avoid refined carbs like white bread and all-purpose flour, as well as sugary baked goods, you should make room for fiber-rich grains to improve digestion and keep you full longer. Such grains include barley, bulgur, couscous, quinoa, and whole wheat.

Indulge in leafy greens and other vegetables that are high in fiber, such as broccoli and carrots, as well as beans and legumes, which can also be great fiber sources. If you are eating a lower-carb diet, you may want to supplement with more green veggies to take advantage of the fiber boost.

Micronutrients

Although it's important to consume the macronutrients—protein, fat, and carbohydrates—micronutrients are just as important for your overall health. And it's easy to miss out on your needed intake, because these nutrients can be hard to track.

Vitamin C is great for immunity, and it can be found in citrus and other fruits. Iron will fight lethargy, so reach for those leafy greens and beef to keep your body strong and energized. Magnesium is important for fighting muscle soreness and improving your mood—common sources include nuts and seeds, avocados, bananas, and leafy greens. Potassium is important for post-workout repair, as it provides electrolytes and hydration, while also repairing and strengthening muscles. You can find potassium in bananas, leafy greens (like spinach, Swiss chard, and kale), and potatoes. Calcium is another important micronutrient—it builds bone density to prevent osteoporosis later in life and also to strengthen bone and muscle mass. Find calcium in Greek yogurt or cottage cheese as well as in green veggies, like broccoli and Brussels sprouts, and in fish, like salmon and canned tuna.

Additionally, you'll need smaller amounts of other nutrients, like copper and manganese, as well as vitamins A and K, and antioxidants to protect your heart, blood health, and bones.

SOURCING QUALITY INGREDIENTS

Clean eating is about picking the right foods and getting them from high-quality, trusted sources. There are many things to consider when purchasing fruits and vegetables, but one good rule of thumb is that if you're going to eat the skin, it should be organic, if possible. For example, avocados and bananas are okay to not buy organic because you don't eat the skins, but berries and peaches are two foods to be aware of because nonorganic fruit is liable to have pesticide residue.

When shopping for fish, go with wild over farmed, as wild fish is more sustainably caught and safer to eat. Plus, a single serving of wild salmon, for example, has half the calories of farmed salmon.

When considering beef, poultry, and eggs, go with grass-fed and organic if possible; these options provide more omega-3s. You want beef that is free of antibiotics and hormones and has been naturally raised, so be sure to check labels. "Natural" alone does not cut it on a label—it has no official definition and is merely a marketing term, so look for specifics like "grass-fed" and similar labels.

Of course, all budgets differ. If you cannot afford organic, you are always better off getting conventionally grown produce over processed foods or take-out. And if organic meat is not a viable option, go with the best product you can afford.

A Clean Kitchen

Having the right tools in your kitchen will make cooking clean, balanced meals easy and simple. For that reason, kitchen prep is the first step in your journey.

To really enjoy a wholesome diet and lifestyle that's abundant in fresh, whole foods boasting ample flavor, you'll need some equipment, pantry staples, fridge and freezer essentials, and clean eating recipes (which you'll find starting in chapter 3—so have no fear).

A well-stocked kitchen also takes the guesswork out of clean eating, as you'll think of meals in simpler terms with the items you already have.

Go-To Pantry Ingredients

There are some ingredients you should always try to keep in your pantry. Having these go-to items on hand can simplify your clean eating plan and make cooking in the kitchen every day a breeze. These ingredients will appear in many of the recipes in this book.

Black pepper and sea salt. Yes, they might seem basic, but they are important for nearly every recipe. Use a pepper grinder for fresh pepper when you need it and use high-quality sea salt.

Broth. With a good broth, like chicken, vegetable, or beef, you can make big-batch soups that you can freeze for later use.

Canned beans. Black, kidney, navy, or white beans are good pantry staples that are super versatile.

Canned fish. Although you can get fresh salmon or keep it frozen for a longer shelf life, canned fish is nicely portioned, and keeps well in your pantry.

Canned tomatoes and tomato sauce. Keep these on hand to use for healthier whole-grain pizzas, a quick pasta sauce, chili, stews, soups, and more. The lycopene found in tomatoes is heart- and skin-protective, too.

Dark chocolate. To satisfy your craving for something sweet, keep dark chocolate stashed in the pantry. It is high in antioxidants and healthier than high-calorie, processed baked goods. Look for a cacao content of 70 percent or higher.

Garlic. Garlic spruces up any dish, and the flavor pairs well with olive oil, citrus, nuts and seeds, and really all proteins, making it super versatile. Keep fresh garlic in the fridge and garlic powder or garlic salt in the pantry for easy access when you need it.

Herbs. Dried basil, thyme, and rosemary add great flavor to dishes without added calories and sugar.

Hot sauce. You can add lots of flavor to foods with hot sauce without a lot of sodium or sugar. As a bonus, the capsaicin in the hot sauce will boost metabolism and suppress appetite. Just check the hot sauce labels to find one that is lower in sodium. There are some that have no sodium, and quite a few that have fewer than 50mg of sodium per teaspoon. Try to stay in that range. You can also use pure ground chiles, which have no sodium (just watch out for chili seasoning, which sometimes can have added salt).

Lentils and chickpeas. Legumes, such as lentils and chickpeas, are as high in fiber and protein as beans but offer different flavor and texture profiles.

Nuts, nut butter, and seeds. Keep nuts, nut butters, and seeds stashed in your pantry for use on the fly. Aim for variety—almonds, pistachios, peanuts, and cashews are excellent nut choices, while almonds or peanuts make great nut butters. For seeds, try pumpkin or sunflower, as well as flax and chia.

Olive and avocado oil. You need cooking oil on hand to stir-fry, roast, grill, or use as a base for dressings and sauces. These two oils have heart-healthy fats to lower inflammation, but they have different smoke points. Use avocado oil for high-heat cooking and olive oil for low-heat cooking or salads.

Essential Tools

For the recipes in this book, you don't need any fancy equipment, just the basics. Beyond the items you probably already have like a skillet, sheet pan, cutting board, measuring cups, and mixing bowls, here are a few other tools that are worth the small investment if you don't already own them:

- Baking pan
- Chef's knife
- Grater
- High-powered blender or food processor
- Ice pop mold (I promise you won't regret this one!)
- Wok

IS THIS CLEAN?

It might be difficult to figure out what qualifies as clean. Yet, by reading the labels and looking out for some "green light" terms or "red flags," you can decipher whether a packaged product is actually healthy or not. Here are some examples:

Cereals. Lots of packaged cereals, oatmeal, granolas, and other grain-based products contain high carb and sugar counts, and for a small portion size. You are better off making your own grain bowl or trail mix at home with whole grains, oats, nuts, dried fruits, and seeds.

Condiments. Many store-bought condiments have sugar, salt, and other additives and oils in them, so you don't want to put these all over your clean, nutritious meal. Instead, DIY your own at home. My go-tos are yogurt-based dips, guacamole, hummus, salsa, pesto, and honey. But if you are buying condiments from the store, make sure they are lower in sugar, unhealthy fats, and sodium.

Farm-raised salmon. Although tasty and more readily available, farmed fish is less healthy than wild; however, it is cheaper and more accessible, so don't worry too much about buying it. Check out the website seafoodwatch.org to find the best options that you can afford.

Nut-based milks. These can be high in sugar and lack essential nutrients, like protein or fiber. Soy milk is a good plant-based milk that's high in protein. Whether you choose nut-based or soy milk, always choose unsweetened varieties.

Tips for Success

It can be a challenge to consistently cook at home when you're new to clean eating. Thankfully, it's a lot easier than you may think, and you can use some shortcuts and meal prep hacks so you can have multiple servings with each recipe and savor the leftovers for a few days (sometimes more), too.

Here are some tips to simplify the process and keep you on track with cooking clean recipes at home:

Meal Prep

Set aside a day of the week (let's say Sunday) to meal prep your week ahead. You can make several Egg White Veggie Cups (page 39) to reheat on busy mornings; pack ready-to-blend ingredients for the Peach Spinach Chia Smoothies (page 47) in resealable bags and store them in the freezer; and make overnight oats and chia seed puddings for on-the-go breakfasts. For lunch and dinner, meal prep baked sweet potatoes, big-batch soups and chilis, and mason jar salads in advance. Chop veggies and proteins and store them in the fridge for stir-fries or a quick sheet pan dinner later in the week.

Shortcuts

There's no need to make everything from scratch. Use your big batch of Smoky Black Bean Chili (page 69) as dinner one night, as a filling for a baked sweet potato the following day, or as a filling for whole wheat tortillas. Got leftover Rainbow Vegetable Scramble (page 41)? Stuff some between a split whole-grain English muffin for a quick breakfast sandwich or throw it into a stir-fry with veggies, protein, and brown rice for a slimmed-down fried rice dish.

Eating Out

Decoding a restaurant menu isn't easy, but here are a few tips. If a dish mentions the words *glazed, crispy, crunchy, candied, coated, creamy,* or, of course, *buttered* or *fried*, it's a red flag and likely not so clean. Instead, go with grilled or roasted, get dressing on the side for salads, and look for more whole food options that are simply prepared.

Cravings

These will come and go—you're only human and are bound to crave something sweet or salty sometimes. You can satisfy cravings with healthier swaps at home. Instead of a candy bar, have Dark Chocolate Avocado Mousse (page 110). Instead of ice cream, make Vanilla N'ice Cream (page 111) with banana.

A CLEAN LIFESTYLE

Living a healthy lifestyle means eating well and staying active—that's why shifting your lifestyle is important, so you can develop clean eating and living habits that'll give you that pep in your step.

To help support your clean eating journey, consider these other habits to boost your healthy new lifestyle:

Exercise regularly. Getting that heart rate up boosts metabolic burn and keeps your cardiovascular system in tip-top shape, thereby lowering the risk of heart disease. Go for aerobic and resistance training for a power combo—you need the cardio for your heart and weight loss/management, while you need resistance training to strengthen muscles and prevent bone density loss.

Manage stress. Stress releases cortisol, the hormone that can wreck your sleeping habits, mood, and appetite. (That's when those cravings spike.) Manage it by doing yoga, meditation, journaling, or exercise for relief throughout the week. Personally, I love boxing and HIIT workouts for both my activity and stress management.

Sleep well. Make sure you get seven to eight hours of sleep every night, as sleep balances hormones and lowers stress, so you can be more productive and make better eating decisions in the week. Think about it: When you don't sleep well, you often wake up craving something fattening and sweet, right? As I mentioned earlier, clean eating will help you sleep better, so once you begin changing how you eat, getting the required zzz's probably won't be a problem.

Avoid environmental toxins. Toxins may appear on GMO-containing or nonorganic foods, often in the form of pesticides, and it's still unclear what their effect on our health will be long-term. Eliminating GMO foods can keep you safer. Shopping sustainably for fish and meat can also reduce the presence of toxic ingredients in the food you eat.

About the Recipes

In part 2, you'll find a variety of recipes that are great for any clean eating beginner, as well as anyone looking to add more nutritious, easy meals to their repertoire. All of the recipes in this book are based on the five clean eating principles I've laid out to set you up for success.

To make the transition into clean eating even simpler, there are icons on the recipes and in each chapter's table of contents that identify those recipes that are especially easy to prepare. The categories are:

 5 INGREDIENTS There are five or fewer ingredients in the recipe (not counting cooking oil, salt, and pepper).

 ONE POT Only one main piece of equipment (such as a skillet, pot, or baking dish) is used.

 QUICK It will take 30 minutes or less to prep and cook the dish.

You'll also find many shortcut tips that will provide guidance on buying and using alternative ingredients. Maybe you'll save money, learn a new food storage tip, or use leftover ingredients wisely in another dish. All of these hacks make clean eating in your kitchen fun and more approachable.

There are also labels to identify dietary concerns, so you can see at glance which recipes are vegan, vegetarian, dairy-free, gluten-free, nut-free, and allergen-free (no dairy, eggs, fish, shellfish, tree nuts, peanuts, wheat, or soy). This makes it easy to whip up a dish that's safe for you and loved ones who may have specific dietary restrictions.

The next chapter features the 21-day meal plan as well as shopping lists for each of the three weeks and prep-ahead lists. Your journey to clean eating has begun!

Penne Primavera, page 74

Chapter Two

21 DAYS OF CLEAN EATING

In this chapter you'll find a 21-day clean eating meal plan that organizes your meals and snacks for the day (and week) with delicious and nutritious recipes—all of which you can make in advance. These ingredients are common and accessible, ones you'll find at your local grocery store. Here's what to know before setting off on your clean eating journey.

About the Meal Plan

This meal plan is designed for those new to clean eating—it won't consume too much time in the kitchen, and you'll be able to make these recipes easily without feeling lost. In the meal plan you'll find:

- Three meals plus one snack per day
- Meals and recipes designed for a single person
- Suggestions for when (and how) to use leftovers from earlier in the week
- Tips for meal prepping ahead of time

There is flexibility on this meal plan, so don't feel obligated to eat certain ingredients you don't enjoy or can't tolerate well.

What to Expect

Upon starting, you might have less energy and more cravings than usual. Why? Your body isn't used to eating these types of foods—and likely in smaller amounts. This is especially true if you're used to ordering take-out food or dining at a restaurant, where the portions are typically large.

Although you may have a rough adjustment with hunger or fatigue the first week, you should feel better by the second week. And by the third week you'll find yourself with *more* energy than you had before starting the clean eating plan. Stick with it—if I can do it, you can, too!

Listening to Your Body

While embarking upon your clean eating journey, always make sure to check in with yourself and your body to see which foods feel and taste good, and which ones may not sit well. Every body is different, and sometimes it takes a bit of trial and error to pinpoint which nutrients you may need more of or which foods may cause indigestion or make you feel lethargic afterward.

All the foods in this meal plan are healthy and clean, so they should perk you up and provide sustainable energy—however, sometimes the body cannot handle ingredients, like nuts, cheese, or certain grains, for example. If you notice adverse effects, swap out an ingredient for something else that's similar (or omit it entirely) and see how you feel.

Now, get ready for a 21-day meal plan that can kick-start your newfound clean eating lifestyle!

WEEK 1

	BREAKFAST	LUNCH	DINNER	SNACK
MONDAY	Avocado Toast with Goat Cheese and Pumpkin Seeds (page 37)	Spicy Chicken Salad Lettuce Wraps (page 94)	Turkey Meatballs with Zucchini Noodles (page 98)	1 cup 0% plain Greek yogurt + 1 tablespoon pistachios
TUESDAY	*Leftover* Avocado Toast with Goat Cheese and Pumpkin Seeds	*Leftover* Turkey Meatballs with Zucchini Noodles	Broiled Salmon with Caponata and Pistachios (page 89)	1 cup cottage cheese + 1 orange
WEDNESDAY	Rainbow Vegetable Scramble (page 41)	*Leftover* Spicy Chicken Salad Lettuce Wraps	Kale Sweet Potato Chickpea Salad (page 64)	1 ounce dark chocolate + 1 tablespoon pistachios
THURSDAY	Chocolate Avocado Smoothies (page 45)	*Leftover* Broiled Salmon with Caponata and Pistachios	Lemon Chicken with Broccoli (page 95)	1 cup cottage cheese + 1 apple
FRIDAY	Egg-Topped Spicy Cauliflower Rice (page 43)	*Leftover* Lemon Chicken with Broccoli inside a baked sweet potato	*Leftover* Kale Sweet Potato Chickpea Salad	1 cup 0% plain Greek yogurt + ½ banana
SATURDAY	*Leftover* Chocolate Avocado Smoothies	*Leftover* Rainbow Vegetable Scramble over Spicy Cauliflower Rice	Chicken Cabbage Roll Skillet (page 97)	1 tablespoon nut butter + 1 cup 0% plain Greek yogurt
SUNDAY	Turkey Sweet Potato Hash (page 44)	*Leftover* Chicken Cabbage Roll Skillet inside a baked sweet potato	Beef Kebabs with Garlic Marinade (page 103)	1 tablespoon nut butter + ½ banana

SHOPPING LIST

PRODUCE

- Apple (1)
- Avocados (3)
- Bananas (2)
- Basil (small bunch)
- Bell peppers, red (5)
- Broccoli florets (2 cups)
- Brussels sprouts (1½ pounds)
- Cabbage (1 small head)
- Carrot (1 medium)
- Cauliflower florets (½ cup)
- Cauliflower rice (6 cups)
- Celery (1 bunch)
- Cilantro (small bunch)
- Garlic (1 large head)
- Ginger (1 inch)
- Jalapeño (1)
- Kale, chopped (6½ cups)
- Lemons (2)
- Lettuce (1 small head)
- Lime (1)
- Mushrooms, sliced (10 ounces)
- Onions, red (2)
- Onions, sweet (2)
- Onion, yellow (1)
- Oregano (small bunch)
- Parsley (small bunch)
- Rosemary (small bunch)
- Scallions (4)
- Spinach, baby (1 ounce)
- Sweet potatoes (6)
- Thyme (small bunch)
- Tomatoes, large (2)
- Tomatoes, medium (2)
- Zucchini noodles (4 cups)

DAIRY AND EGGS

- Cottage cheese (2 cups)
- Eggs (9)
- Goat cheese, crumbled (1 ounce)
- Milk, almond, unsweetened (2 cups)
- Yogurt, Greek, 0% plain (3¾ cups)

MEAT AND POULTRY

- Beef, sirloin steak (8 ounces)
- Chicken, 2 (5-ounce) boneless, skinless breasts
- Chicken breast, cooked, or rotisserie chicken (12 ounces)
- Chicken, ground, extra-lean (8 ounces)
- Turkey breast, ground, extra-lean (2 pounds)

SEAFOOD

- Salmon, 2 (5-ounce) fillets

PANTRY: CANNED AND BOTTLED

- Broth, low-sodium chicken
- Chickpeas, no-salt-added, 1 (15-ounce) can
- Maple syrup
- Olive oil, extra-virgin
- Olives, chopped
- Roasted red peppers
- Tomatoes, crushed, 1 (15-ounce) can
- Tomatoes, no-salt-added diced, 1 (28-ounce) can
- Vanilla extract, pure
- Vinegar, apple cider
- Vinegar, balsamic

PANTRY: DRY GOODS

- Almond flour
- Almonds, slivered
- Bread, whole-grain
- Chocolate, dark (1 ounce)
- Chocolate protein powder
- Cocoa powder, unsweetened
- Pistachios
- Pumpkin seeds
- Raisins

PANTRY: HERBS AND SPICES

- Black pepper
- Cayenne pepper
- Chipotle chile powder
- Coriander, ground
- Cumin, ground
- Curry powder
- Red pepper flakes
- Sea salt

PREP AHEAD

1. Prep the smoothies by filling freezer bags with the measured-out ingredients. Store in the freezer until ready.
2. Bake the sweet potatoes and stash in the fridge for later use.
3. Prepare the Avocado Yogurt Dressing (page 126) and keep in the fridge to have on hand.
4. Chop the veggies for the Rainbow Vegetable Scramble and store in containers in the fridge.
5. If making your own zucchini noodles (rather than using store-bought) for the Turkey Meatballs with Zucchini Noodles, spiralize the zucchini and store in a container in the fridge.

WEEK 2

	BREAKFAST	LUNCH	DINNER	SNACK
MONDAY	Egg White Veggie Cups (page 39)	Tofu Mango Bowls (page 65)	Sheet Pan Shrimp with Vegetables (page 85)	1 cup 0% plain Greek yogurt + 1 cup chopped mango
TUESDAY	*Leftover* Egg White Veggie Cups	*Leftover* Tofu Mango Bowls	Penne Primavera (page 74)	1 apple + 1 tablespoon peanut butter
WEDNESDAY	Peanut Butter Chia Seed Pudding (page 38)	*Leftover* Penne Primavera	Ground Beef and Veggie Skillet (page 101)	½ grapefruit + 1 cup 0% plain Greek yogurt
THURSDAY	*Leftover* Egg White Veggie Cups	*Leftover* Ground Beef and Veggie Skillet	Spicy Tofu Tacos (page 70)	*Leftover* Peanut Butter Chia Seed Pudding
FRIDAY	*Leftover* Spicy Tofu Tacos	Spinach Grapefruit Salad with Broiled Shrimp (page 80)	*Leftover* Ground Beef and Veggie Skillet	1 cup cottage cheese + 1 apple, diced
SATURDAY	*Leftover* Peanut Butter Chia Seed Pudding	*Leftover* Ground Beef and Veggie Skillet	Beef Kebabs with Garlic Marinade (page 103)	½ grapefruit + 1 hard-boiled egg
SUNDAY	*Leftover* Egg White Veggie Cups	*Leftover* Sheet Pan Shrimp with Vegetables	*Leftover* Spinach Grapefruit Salad with Broiled Shrimp	*Leftover* Peanut Butter Chia Seed Pudding

SHOPPING LIST

PRODUCE

- Apples (2)
- Asparagus (1 pound)
- Avocados (2)
- Basil (small bunch)
- Bell peppers, red (3)
- Bell peppers, yellow (2)
- Bok choy (1 small head)
- Broccoli (1 head)
- Brussels sprouts (10 ounces)
- Carrots (3)
- Celery (1 bunch)
- Cilantro (small bunch)
- Garlic (2 heads)
- Grapefruit, ruby red (1)
- Grapefruit, yellow (1)
- Green beans (4 ounces)
- Jalapeño (1)
- Kale, shredded (½ cup)
- Lemons (4)
- Lettuce (1 small head)
- Limes (2)
- Mangos (2)
- Mushrooms, white (1 pound)
- Onion, red (1)
- Onions, sweet, medium (2)
- Onions, sweet, small (2)
- Orange (1)
- Parsley (small bunch)
- Raspberries (½ pint)
- Rosemary (small bunch)
- Scallions (2)
- Spinach, baby (4 ounces)
- Thyme (small bunch)
- Tomatoes, cherry (10 ounces)
- Tomatoes, large (3)
- Zucchini (2)

DAIRY AND EGGS

- Cheese, feta (2 ounces)
- Cheese, mozzarella, shredded (2 ounces)
- Cheese, Parmesan, grated (1 ounce)
- Cottage cheese (8 ounces)
- Eggs (1½ dozen)
- Milk, vanilla almond, unsweetened (2 cups)
- Tofu, extra-firm (21 ounces)
- Yogurt, Greek, 0% plain (24 ounces)

MEAT

- Beef, ground, 97% lean (1 pound)
- Beef, sirloin steak (8 ounces)

SEAFOOD

- Shrimp, large (31/35 count), peeled and deveined (1 pound)

FROZEN

- Edamame, shelled (½ cup)

PANTRY: CANNED AND BOTTLED

- Broth, low-sodium vegetable
- Olive oil spray
- Olive oil
- Peanut butter
- Sesame oil
- Vanilla extract, pure
- Vinegar, apple cider

PANTRY: DRY GOODS

- Cashews
- Chia seeds (½ cup)
- Chocolate, dark (2 ounces)
- Hemp hearts
- Penne, whole-grain (4 ounces)
- Taco shells, corn (8)

PANTRY: HERBS AND SPICES

- Bay leaves
- Black pepper
- Cayenne pepper
- Chili powder
- Cinnamon, ground
- Coriander, ground
- Cumin, ground
- Garlic powder
- Italian seasoning
- Onion powder
- Paprika, smoked
- Peppercorns
- Red pepper flakes
- Sea salt

PREP AHEAD

1. Prepare the Egg White Veggie Cups in bulk and store in a sealed container in the freezer for the week.
2. Prepare the Peanut Butter Chia Seed Pudding and let it soak overnight.

WEEK 3

	BREAKFAST	LUNCH	DINNER	SNACK
MONDAY	Peach Spinach Chia Smoothies (page 47)	Baked sweet potato + 4 ounces store-bought cooked salmon + 1 tablespoon goat cheese	Sheet Pan Steak Fajitas (page102)	1 cup chopped peaches + 1 cup 0% plain Greek yogurt
TUESDAY	Egg-Topped Spicy Cauliflower Rice (page 43)	*Leftover* Sheet Pan Steak Fajitas	Brussels Sprouts with Cumin and Sunflower Seeds (page 56) + 4 ounces store-bought cooked salmon	1 cup cottage cheese + "Cheesy" Kale Chips (page 51)
WEDNESDAY	*Leftover* Brussels Sprouts with Cumin and Sunflower Seeds + 3 scrambled eggs	Baja Halibut Tacos with Lime (page 81)	Falafel Baby Green Salad (page 67)	1 slice whole-grain toast + 1 tablespoon peanut butter
THURSDAY	Avocado Toast with Goat Cheese and Pumpkin Seeds (page 37)	*Leftover* Falafel Baby Green Salad	Veggie Bean Sprout Chow Mein (page 72) topped with 1 fried egg	1 cup 0% plain Greek yogurt + 1 banana, sliced
FRIDAY	*Leftover* Avocado Toast with Goat Cheese and Pumpkin Seeds	1 baked sweet potato + 4 ounces store-bought cooked salmon	*Leftover* Sheet Pan Steak Fajitas	1 cup cottage cheese + 1 cup chopped peaches
SATURDAY	*Leftover* Peach Spinach Chia Smoothies	*Leftover* Veggie Bean Sprout Chow Mein	*Leftover* Falafel Baby Green Salad	*Leftover* "Cheesy" Kale Chips + 4 thin slices lean deli turkey breast
SUNDAY	*Leftover* Brussels Sprouts with Cumin and Sunflower Seeds + 1 slice whole-grain toast + 1 tablespoon peanut butter	*Leftover* Falafel Baby Green Salad	*Leftover* Baja Halibut Tacos with Lime	1 banana + 1 tablespoon peanut butter

SHOPPING LIST

PRODUCE

- Avocados (2)
- Bananas (2)
- Bean sprouts (8 ounces)
- Bell peppers, green (2)
- Bell peppers, red (2)
- Bok choy (1 small head)
- Broccoli florets (8 ounces)
- Brussels sprouts (1 pound)
- Cabbage, red (1 small head)
- Carrots (2)
- Cauliflower rice (4 cups)
- Cilantro (small bunch)
- Cucumber (1)
- Garlic (1 small head)
- Ginger (1 inch)
- Greens, mixed baby (6 ounces)
- Kale, chopped (4 cups)
- Lemon (1)
- Lettuce, butter (1 small head)
- Limes (3)
- Onion, sweet (1)
- Onion, yellow (1)
- Parsley (small bunch)
- Peaches (2)
- Scallion (1)
- Snow peas (1 cup)
- Spinach, chopped (2 ounces)
- Sweet potatoes (2)
- Tomatoes, cherry (6 ounces)
- Tomatoes, large (3)
- Tomato, medium (1)

DAIRY AND EGGS

- Cottage cheese (2 cups)
- Eggs (1 dozen)
- Goat cheese (2 ounces)
- Milk, nondairy (2 cups)
- Yogurt, Greek, 0% plain (2⅓ cups)

MEAT AND POULTRY

- Beef, sirloin steak (12 ounces)
- Turkey breast, deli (4 thin slices)

SEAFOOD

- Halibut fillet (8 ounces)
- Salmon, cooked (12 ounces)

FROZEN

- Peaches, sliced (1 cup)

PANTRY: CANNED AND BOTTLED

- Chickpeas, no-salt-added, 1 (15-ounce) can
- Olive oil
- Olive oil spray
- Peanut butter
- Sesame oil
- Sriracha sauce
- Tamari, reduced-sodium

PANTRY: DRY GOODS

- Almond flour
- Bread, whole-grain
- Cashews
- Chia seeds
- Nutritional yeast
- Protein powder, unsweetened vanilla
- Pumpkin seeds
- Sesame seeds
- Sunflower seeds, roasted
- Tortillas, soft corn, 4 (6-inch)

PANTRY: HERBS AND SPICES

- Black pepper
- Chili powder
- Chipotle chile powder
- Coriander, ground
- Cumin, ground
- Fajita seasoning
- Paprika, smoked
- Sea salt

PREP AHEAD

1. Prepare your smoothie freezer packs so they are ready for immediate blending on Monday morning. Keep the rest of the bags in the freezer for the remainder of the week.
2. Bake the sweet potatoes for lunches so they are easy to heat up and eat during the week.

Part Two

75 CLEAN RECIPES

Egg-Topped Spicy Cauliflower Rice, page 43

Chapter Three
BREAKFASTS AND SMOOTHIES

Almond Butter, Blueberry, and Pistachio Overnight Oats ⚙️⬭

You can prepare this breakfast overnight, so it's ready to grab and go come morning. And trust me—this meal prep will come in handy on those busy mornings when you don't have the time to whip up something. Nutty and fruit-focused, this filling recipe is packed with heart-healthy fats and protein from all-natural almond butter as well as a rich dose of fiber from pistachios and blueberries.

DAIRY-FREE **VEGAN**
GLUTEN-FREE

Prep time: 10 minutes, plus overnight to soak
Serves 2

1 cup unsweetened
  nondairy milk, plus more
  if desired
2 tablespoons natural
  almond butter
1 cup gluten-free
  rolled oats
½ cup blueberries
¼ cup chopped pistachios

1. Divide the milk and almond butter between two mason jars or sealable containers and stir until blended. Divide the oats, blueberries, and pistachios between the jars. Stir, seal, and refrigerate overnight.

2. In the morning, stir the mixture and adjust the thickness with more milk, if desired.

TIP: For a thicker texture and a protein boost, add 1 teaspoon chia seeds to each jar along with the other ingredients.

Per serving: Calories: 356; Protein: 12g; Carbohydrates: 40g; Fiber: 8g; Total fat: 19g; Saturated fat: 2g; Sugar: 6.5g; Sodium: 93mg

Avocado Toast with Goat Cheese and Pumpkin Seeds ⊛⊖⊘

Avocado toast is a no-brainer for a wholesome breakfast that's simple to prepare. The type of toast matters: for gut health, digestion, and satiety, a whole-grain, whole wheat, or nutritiously dense gluten-free bread is preferred over white bread. Toasted pumpkin seeds and an extra squeeze of lemon juice add a wonderful flavor punch.

NUT-FREE   **VEGETARIAN**

Prep time: 10 minutes
Cook time: 5 minutes
Serves 2

1 avocado, halved
   and pitted
2 teaspoons fresh lemon
   juice, plus more for
   serving (optional)
Sea salt
Freshly ground
   black pepper
2 slices whole-grain
   bread, toasted
2 tablespoons crumbled
   soft goat cheese
2 tablespoons pumpkin
   seeds, toasted

1. Scoop the avocado into a small bowl. Add the lemon juice, season lightly with salt and pepper, and mash everything together.

2. Divide the mashed avocado between the toast slices and top each with 1 tablespoon of goat cheese and 1 tablespoon of pumpkin seeds. Spritz with a little lemon juice, if desired.

TIP: You can swap out the goat cheese and pumpkin seeds for feta, roasted red pepper, sun-dried tomatoes, chia seeds, or chopped hard-boiled egg.

Per serving: Calories: 290; Protein: 11g; Carbohydrates: 25g; Fiber: 7g; Total fat: 19g; Saturated fat: 4.5g; Sugar: 3g; Sodium: 236mg

Peanut Butter Chia Seed Pudding ⊖

Here's another breakfast that can be prepared overnight to make mornings a breeze. The pudding soaks and chills overnight in the refrigerator. If you prepare this pudding in a mason jar, you can take it with you on your commute. For some added sweetness, chop up dark chocolate and sprinkle it on top. The darker the chocolate, the greater its antioxidant content.

DAIRY-FREE | **VEGAN**
GLUTEN-FREE

Prep time: 10 minutes, plus overnight to chill
Serves 4

2 cups unsweetened
 vanilla almond milk,
 at room temperature
3 tablespoons natural
 peanut butter
1 teaspoon pure
 vanilla extract
¼ teaspoon ground
 cinnamon
½ cup chia seeds
1 cup raspberries
¼ cup chopped dark
 chocolate (optional)
2 tablespoons
 hemp hearts

1. In a medium bowl, whisk together the almond milk, peanut butter, vanilla, and cinnamon until blended. Add the chia seeds and stir until combined. Cover and refrigerate overnight.

2. Stir the mixture in the morning and transfer to serving bowls. Top with raspberries, dark chocolate (if using), and hemp hearts and serve. Store the pudding, without the toppings, in a sealed container in the refrigerator for up to 3 days.

TIP: If you prefer a smoother pudding, combine the milk, peanut butter, vanilla, cinnamon, and chia seeds in a blender and blend until smooth. Refrigerate overnight and add any desired toppings.

Per serving: Calories: 234; Protein: 9g; Carbohydrates: 16g; Fiber: 11g; Total fat: 16g; Saturated fat: 2g; Sugar: 3g; Sodium: 140mg

Egg White Veggie Cups

These cups are made in a muffin pan, and they are packed with protein, fiber, and antioxidants. Egg whites contain protein but not brain-boosting choline, which is only found in yolks. If you are not generally watching your cholesterol (or you haven't been told by your cardiologist to avoid yolks), feel free to use whole eggs. You'll need about 10 large eggs.

GLUTEN-FREE **VEGETARIAN** **NUT-FREE**

Prep time: 15 minutes
Cook time: 20 minutes
Makes 12 cups

Olive oil spray
15 large egg whites
½ cup shredded kale
½ cup chopped white mushrooms
½ cup chopped red bell pepper
½ cup shredded part-skim mozzarella cheese
1 tablespoon chopped fresh parsley
¼ teaspoon sea salt
⅛ teaspoon freshly ground black pepper

1. Preheat the oven to 350°F. Lightly mist a 12-cup muffin pan with olive oil spray.

2. In a large bowl, whisk together the egg whites, kale, mushrooms, red bell pepper, mozzarella, parsley, salt, and pepper.

3. Divide the egg mixture equally among the muffin cups. Bake for 20 minutes, or until the egg whites are fully cooked.

4. Let the egg muffins cool for about 5 minutes. Run a knife around the edges to loosen them from the cups and serve.

5. Store the cooled muffins in a resealable plastic bag in the refrigerator for up to 4 days or in the freezer for up to 1 month.

TIP: You can also cook this dish in a 9-inch round baking dish, sprayed with cooking spray. Bake for 40 to 45 minutes, cut into wedges, and serve.

Per serving (2 cups): Calories: 107; Protein: 14g; Carbohydrates: 2g; Fiber: 0.5g; Total fat: 5g; Saturated fat: 1g; Sugar: 1.5g; Sodium: 329mg

Chocolate Protein Pancakes ⚡

Pancakes don't have to be a carb and sugar overload. This recipe helps you avoid that dreaded midmorning sugar crash by calling for unsweetened applesauce. The no-sugar-added chocolate protein powder and the cinnamon and nutmeg provide a nice balance of sweet and savory.

DAIRY-FREE **NUT-FREE**
GLUTEN-FREE **VEGETARIAN**

Prep time: 10 minutes
Cook time: 10 minutes
Serves 4

4 large eggs
¾ cup unsweetened
    applesauce
½ cup gluten-free
    rolled oats
⅓ cup unsweetened
    chocolate protein
    powder
2 tablespoons
    unsweetened
    cocoa powder
½ teaspoon ground
    cinnamon
¼ teaspoon
    ground nutmeg
Olive oil spray

1. In a blender, combine the eggs, applesauce, oats, protein powder, cocoa powder, cinnamon, and nutmeg and pulse until smooth.

2. Heat a large skillet over medium heat and mist with olive oil spray. Pour the batter into the skillet using a ¼-cup measure. There should be room for 4 pancakes. Spread out the batter using the back of a spoon. Cook the pancakes for about 2 minutes, or until golden and bubbles form on the tops. Flip the pancakes and cook until there is no longer any wet batter, about 1 minute.

3. Transfer the pancakes to a plate, cover loosely with aluminum foil, and repeat with the remaining batter.

4. Serve warm. Store leftovers in a sealed container in the refrigerator for up to 3 days.

TIP: These pancakes are also delicious served cold with a little almond butter.

Per serving: Calories: 180; Protein: 15g; Carbohydrates: 14g; Fiber: 3g; Total fat: 7.5g; Saturated fat: 2g; Sugar: 7g; Sodium: 77mg

Rainbow Vegetable Scramble ⬭⚡

An egg scramble makes an easy weekday breakfast, and this one has a variety of bright veggies for an antioxidant boost. You can keep the egg yolk for its choline benefits, or you can ditch it and go with an egg white scramble instead (you'll need 6 large egg whites). Season the scramble with hot sauce if you like a little spice.

DAIRY-FREE **NUT-FREE**
GLUTEN-FREE **VEGETARIAN**

Prep time: 15 minutes
Cook time: 15 minutes
Serves 2

4 large eggs
2 tablespoons
  unsweetened
  nondairy milk
1 teaspoon olive oil
½ cup sliced white
  mushrooms
1 red bell pepper, chopped
½ cup small cauliflower
  florets
¼ cup shredded carrot
½ cup chopped kale
1 scallion, green part
  only, chopped
Sea salt
Freshly ground
  black pepper

1. In a small bowl, whisk together the eggs and milk until well combined. Set aside.

2. In a large nonstick skillet, heat the oil over medium-high heat. Add the mushrooms and sauté for about 5 minutes, or until tender. Add the bell pepper, cauliflower, and carrot and sauté for about 6 minutes, or until tender. Add the kale and scallion greens and sauté for 2 minutes.

3. Move the vegetables to the side of the skillet and pour in the eggs. Scramble the eggs for about 2 minutes, or until fluffy curds form.

4. Remove the skillet from the heat and stir the vegetables into the scrambled eggs. Season lightly with salt and pepper and serve.

TIP: Instead of eggs, swap in 14 ounces of crumbled extra-firm tofu for a tasty vegan option. The cook time will be the same.

Per serving: Calories: 202; Protein: 15g; Carbohydrates: 8g; Fiber: 2.5g; Total fat: 12g; Saturated fat: 3.5g; Sugar: 4g; Sodium: 250mg

Southwestern Egg Bake

An egg bake is awesome for meal prepping. This high-protein breakfast has a Southwestern flair by way of Monterey Jack cheese, onion, avocado, jalapeño, and chopped fresh cilantro. White beans provide fiber. Make sure to rinse the beans before cooking to remove any excess sodium used in the canning process.

Prep time: 10 minutes
Cook time: 25 minutes
Serves 4

Olive oil spray
8 large eggs
¼ cup unsweetened
   almond milk
8 tablespoons shred-
   ded Monterey Jack
   cheese, divided
1 teaspoon olive oil
¼ small red
   onion, chopped
½ jalapeño pepper,
   seeded and chopped
1 cup canned white beans,
   drained and rinsed
12 cherry tomatoes,
   quartered
1 avocado, peeled, pitted,
   and chopped
2 tablespoons chopped
   fresh cilantro

1. Preheat the oven to 350°F. Lightly mist an 8-inch round baking dish with olive oil spray.

2. In a small bowl, beat together the eggs, milk, and 3 tablespoons of Monterey Jack until well blended.

3. In a medium skillet, heat the oil over medium-high heat. Add the onion and jalapeño and sauté for about 4 minutes, or until softened. Spread the sautéed onion and jalapeño and the beans in the prepared baking dish and pour in the egg mixture. Scatter the cherry tomatoes and remaining 5 tablespoons of Monterey Jack evenly over the eggs.

4. Bake for 20 to 25 minutes until the eggs are lightly browned and puffed.

5. Serve topped with the avocado and cilantro.

TIP: If you want, pair with a slice of whole-grain or whole wheat toast. If you're not into the heat, omit the jalapeño and go with some fresh herbs instead.

Per serving: Calories: 353; Protein: 22g; Carbohydrates: 21g; Fiber: 6g; Total fat: 21g; Saturated fat: 6.5g; Sugar: 2g; Sodium: 467mg

Egg-Topped Spicy Cauliflower Rice ⚡

Cauliflower rice is a low-carb rice alternative to white rice that can really do no wrong. Mild in flavor, cauliflower can complement the flavors in any dish, plus it's packed with nutrients. Prep a large batch of cauliflower rice at the beginning of the week to keep in the fridge as a simple base for hearty bowls and salads or as a side for protein at dinner. This recipe features both herby and spicy elements.

DAIRY-FREE **NUT-FREE**
GLUTEN-FREE **VEGETARIAN**

Prep time: 15 minutes
Cook time: 10 minutes
Serves 4

2 tablespoons olive
  oil, divided
4 cups cauliflower rice
1 teaspoon minced garlic
1 teaspoon ground cumin
¼ teaspoon chipotle
  chile powder
¼ teaspoon sea salt
2 large tomatoes,
  chopped
Juice of ½ lime
1 tablespoon chopped
  fresh cilantro
4 large eggs
Freshly ground
  black pepper

1. In a large nonstick skillet, heat 1 tablespoon of oil over medium heat. Add the cauliflower, garlic, cumin, chipotle powder, and salt and sauté for about 3 minutes, or until the cauliflower is slightly soft and the spices are evenly distributed.

2. Add the tomatoes, lime juice, and cilantro and cook for 1 minute. Scrape the mixture into a bowl, partially cover, and set aside.

3. Wipe out the skillet and heat the remaining 1 tablespoon of oil over medium heat. Crack each egg into a small bowl and then add them one at a time to the skillet. Cover with a lid and cook for 2 to 2½ minutes until the whites are set. Season the eggs with pepper.

4. Divide the cauliflower rice equally among four plates. Top each with 1 egg and serve. Refrigerate leftover cauliflower rice in a sealed container for up to 2 days.

TIP: Scrambled or poached eggs would be lovely on this savory rice.

Per serving: Calories: 180; Protein: 9g; Carbohydrates: 8g; Fiber: 3g; Total fat: 12g; Saturated fat: 2.5g; Sugar: 4.5g; Sodium: 246mg

Turkey Sweet Potato Hash

Ground turkey breast adds lean protein to this hash. Sweet potatoes provide antioxidants like beta-carotene to promote eye, skin, and heart health. You can use white potatoes if you prefer. Both types of potato offer rich potassium to promote proper electrolyte balance and hydration and to help repair damaged muscles post-exercise.

ALLERGEN-FREE **GLUTEN-FREE**
DAIRY-FREE **NUT-FREE**

Prep time: 15 minutes
Cook time: 20 minutes
Serves 4

1 tablespoon olive oil
1 pound extra-lean ground
   turkey breast
½ sweet onion, chopped
1 teaspoon minced garlic
2 sweet potatoes,
   peeled and cut into
   ½-inch chunks
10 to 12 Brussels sprouts,
   trimmed and quartered
1 red bell pepper, chopped
2 teaspoons chopped
   fresh thyme
Pinch sea salt
Pinch freshly ground
   black pepper

1. In a large skillet, heat the oil over medium-high heat. Add the turkey and sauté for about 8 minutes, or until cooked through. Using a slotted spoon, transfer the turkey to a plate and set aside.

2. Add the onion and garlic to the skillet and sauté for about 3 minutes, or until softened. Add the sweet potatoes, Brussels sprouts, bell pepper, and thyme and sauté for about 10 minutes, or until the vegetables are tender.

3. Return the turkey to the skillet, along with any juices from the plate, and toss to combine. Season lightly with salt and pepper and serve. Store leftovers in a sealed container in the refrigerator for up to 3 days.

TIP: You could also make this with 3 cups chopped leftover cooked turkey instead of ground. Add the cooked turkey after the veggies are cooked and toss until heated through.

Per serving: Calories: 253; Protein: 31g; Carbohydrates: 23g; Fiber: 5g; Total fat: 4.5g; Saturated fat: 1g; Sugar: 7g; Sodium: 206mg

Chocolate Avocado Smoothies ⊜⚡

Chocolate for breakfast? Yes—it's totally possible when combined with an abundance of greens, like iron-dense baby spinach and avocado, which boast heart-healthy fats, fiber, and magnesium. You can make smoothie packs and store them in the freezer. All you have to do is dump the contents into a high-powered blender.

DAIRY-FREE **VEGAN**
GLUTEN-FREE

Prep time: 10 minutes
Serves 2

1 avocado, halved
   and pitted
2 cups unsweetened
   almond milk
1 cup baby spinach
1 banana
1 scoop unsweetened
   chocolate protein powder
1 tablespoon unsweetened
   cocoa powder
1 teaspoon pure
   vanilla extract
1 teaspoon maple syrup
   (optional)

Scoop the avocado into a blender. Add the almond milk, spinach, banana, protein powder, cocoa powder, vanilla, and maple syrup (if using) and blend until smooth. Serve immediately.

TIP: This also makes a nice smoothie bowl topped with fresh raspberries, cacao nibs, unsweetened shredded coconut, and toasted or raw pumpkin seeds.

Per serving: Calories: 236; Protein: 13g; Carbohydrates: 11g; Fiber: 7g; Total fat: 16g; Saturated fat: 1.5g; Sugar: 0.5g; Sodium: 220mg

Muesli Blueberry Smoothies ⬭⚡

This fruity smoothie uses gluten-free rolled oats. The Greek yogurt provides probiotics, which improve gut health and boost immunity as well as keep you regular. To keep the sugar low, it's made with plain Greek yogurt and unsweetened almond milk, but the blueberries and banana make it plenty sweet.

GLUTEN-FREE **VEGETARIAN**

Prep time: 10 minutes
Serves 2

1 cup unsweetened
  almond milk
½ cup 0% plain
  Greek yogurt
½ cup gluten-free
  rolled oats
1 cup frozen blueberries
1 banana
½ teaspoon pure
  vanilla extract

In a blender, combine the almond milk, yogurt, oats, blueberries, banana, and vanilla and blend until smooth. Serve immediately.

TIP: Blueberries are particularly beneficial for cognitive health and the prevention of Alzheimer's disease and dementia, so having them in the morning could do wonders for your brain health in addition to your taste buds.

Per serving: Calories: 215; Protein: 10g; Carbohydrates: 37g; Fiber: 5.5g; Total fat: 3.5g; Saturated fat: 0.5g; Sugar: 15g; Sodium: 118mg

Peach Spinach Chia Smoothies ⊛⊝⚡

This gluten-free smoothie gets natural sweetness from peaches as well as iron and protein from greens. What's more, the chia seeds provide ample fiber and healthy omega-3 fatty acids. Go with almond, oat, soy, or any nondairy milk of your choosing. If you're looking to increase the smoothie's protein content and allergies are not a concern, go with soy milk.

DAIRY-FREE   **VEGAN**
GLUTEN-FREE

Prep time: 10 minutes
Serves 2

2 cups unsweetened
   nondairy milk
2 cups roughly
   chopped spinach
1 cup frozen
   sliced peaches
2 scoops unsweetened
   vanilla protein powder
2 tablespoons chia seeds

In a blender, combine the milk, spinach, peaches, protein powder, and chia seeds and blend until very smooth. Serve immediately.

TIP: If you don't have protein powder, add 1 cup 0% plain Greek yogurt for a delicious and tart protein-packed treat.

Per serving: Calories: 252; Protein: 23g; Carbohydrates: 15g; Fiber: 6g; Total fat: 12g; Saturated fat: 1g; Sugar: 6g; Sodium: 225mg

Chicken Veggie Lettuce Rolls, page 53

Chapter Four
SNACKS AND SIDES

Avocado Hummus ⬭⚡

Hummus is an easy snack-time staple, and it's an awesome party dish. This recipe is jazzed up with the addition of heart-healthy avocado to the chickpea base. If you like your dip well spiced, add more cumin and maybe some hot sauce or minced jalapeño. Serve the dip with whole-grain pitas or fresh veggies.

DAIRY-FREE **VEGAN**
GLUTEN-FREE

Prep time: 10 minutes
Serves 4

1 avocado, halved
   and pitted
1 (15-ounce) can no-salt-
   added chickpeas,
   drained and rinsed
1 tablespoon tahini
2 teaspoons minced garlic
Juice of 1 lemon
1 teaspoon ground cumin
Sea salt
1 tablespoon pine
   nuts, toasted

1. Scoop the avocado into a blender. Add the chickpeas, tahini, garlic, lemon juice, and cumin and pulse, scraping down the sides at least once, until very smooth.

2. Transfer the mixture to a bowl, season lightly with salt, and top with a scattering of pine nuts. Refrigerate any leftover dip in a sealed container for up to 5 days.

TIP: Any legume is fabulous in hummus, so try lentils, navy beans, black beans, or kidney beans for different textures and tastes.

Per serving: Calories: 174; Protein: 6g; Carbohydrates: 20g; Fiber: 7g; Total fat: 9g; Saturated fat: 1g; Sugar: 2g; Sodium: 51mg

"Cheesy" Kale Chips ✦

Most packaged chips (especially the ones with cheese) are high in calories, unhealthy fats, sodium, and refined sugars. And they lack any real nutrition. The solution? Grab some greens, like kale, and make chips using nutritional yeast. If you love real dairy, feel free to use a finely grated cheese such as Parmesan or Pecorino Romano.

ALLERGEN-FREE **NUT-FREE**
DAIRY-FREE **VEGAN**
GLUTEN-FREE

Prep time: 15 minutes
Cook time: 25 minutes
Serves 2

4 cups 2-inch pieces torn kale (from about 6 large leaves, stemmed and deribbed)
1 tablespoon olive oil
¼ teaspoon sea salt
1 tablespoon nutritional yeast

1. Preheat the oven to 300°F. Line a baking sheet with parchment paper.

2. In a large bowl, combine the kale, oil, and salt and use your fingers to thoroughly rub the oil into each piece.

3. Spread the kale in a single layer on the prepared baking sheet.

4. Bake for 10 minutes. Turn the kale and bake for another 10 to 15 minutes until crispy and dry.

5. Transfer the chips to a rack, sprinkle with the nutritional yeast, and cool completely.

6. Although best eaten fresh, these chips can be stored in a sealed container at room temperature for up to 3 days.

TIP: Season the chips with your favorite herbs and spices. Try cumin, Italian seasoning, garam masala, or even cayenne pepper for a kick of heat.

Per serving: Calories: 83; Protein: 2g; Carbohydrates: 3g; Fiber: 1.5g; Total fat: 7g; Saturated fat: 1g; Sugar: 1g; Sodium: 306mg

Barbecue-Style Roasted Chickpeas

This recipe uses classic barbecue seasonings but with healthier ingredients to whip up a better-for-you snack option that has all the smokiness you crave but with a nutritional boost. This snack is not only super crispy but also high in protein and fiber.

Prep time: 10 minutes, plus 30 minutes to dry
Cook time: 45 minutes
Makes about 3⅓ cups

2 (15-ounce) cans no-salt-added chickpeas, drained and rinsed
1 tablespoon olive oil
2 teaspoons smoked paprika
1 teaspoon chili powder
1 teaspoon garlic powder
½ teaspoon ground cumin
½ teaspoon onion powder
½ teaspoon sea salt

1. Spread the chickpeas out on paper towels to dry for about 30 minutes.

2. Preheat the oven to 375°F. Line a baking sheet with parchment paper.

3. In a large bowl, combine the chickpeas, oil, smoked paprika, chili powder, garlic powder, cumin, onion powder, and salt and toss until evenly coated.

4. Spread the chickpeas in a single layer on the prepared baking sheet.

5. Bake for 20 minutes. Toss the chickpeas and continue to bake for another 20 to 25 minutes until golden and crisp.

6. Let the chickpeas cool completely, then serve. Store leftovers in a sealed container at room temperature for up to 5 days.

TIP: Make sure you thoroughly dry the chickpeas so the oil can coat them evenly, which will ensure a lovely crispy snack.

Per serving (⅔ cup): Calories: 168; Protein: 7g; Carbohydrates: 24g; Fiber: 7g; Total fat: 5g; Saturated fat: 0.5g; Sugar: 2.5g; Sodium: 245mg

Chicken Veggie Lettuce Rolls

Lettuce serves as the perfect chicken and veggie wrapper: no grease, sodium, carbs, or gluten. This recipe's peanut sauce complements the aromatic notes of the rolls, so feel free to dunk with abandon. Yum!

DAIRY-FREE   **GLUTEN-FREE**

Prep time: 45 minutes
Makes 8 rolls

8 large Boston lettuce
  leaves
1 cup shredded cooked
  chicken breast (left-
  overs or store-bought
  rotisserie)
1 large carrot, cut into
  matchsticks
1 English cucumber, cut
  into matchsticks
1 red bell pepper, cut into
  thin strips
¼ cup shredded
  red cabbage
¼ cup radish matchsticks
2 tablespoons chopped
  fresh cilantro
Thai-Inspired Peanut
  Sauce (page 125),
  for dipping

1. Place a lettuce leaf on a clean work surface. On the bottom third of the leaf, arrange 2 tablespoons of chicken, and one-eighth of the carrot, cucumber, bell pepper, cabbage, radish, and cilantro. Fold the bottom of the leaf over the filling, then fold in each side firmly over the bottom fold. Then, roll up the wrap away from you, tightly tucking the filling in as you go. Secure the roll with a toothpick and set aside.

2. Repeat with the remaining leaves and filling ingredients and serve with the peanut sauce.

3. Store leftovers, wrapped in plastic wrap, in the refrigerator for up to 2 days.

TIP: You can roll these up without tucking in the sides. It won't be as pretty but will still taste spectacular.

Per serving (1 roll): Calories: 156; Protein: 11g; Carbohydrates: 7g; Fiber: 2g; Total fat: 10g; Saturated fat: 1.5g; Sugar: 3g; Sodium: 206mg

PB&J Bars

This twist on the classic sandwich combo packs a nutrition punch. Protein powder provides protein, and rolled oats and pumpkin seeds provide fiber and complex carbs to energize you. When you're stuck in an afternoon slump, grab one of these bars and bounce right back.

DAIRY-FREE **VEGAN**
GLUTEN-FREE

Prep time: 10 minutes, plus 1 hour to chill
Makes 10 bars

1 cup natural
    peanut butter
¼ cup maple syrup
1 teaspoon pure
    vanilla extract
1 cup gluten-free rolled
    oats, plus more if needed
¼ cup unsweetened
    vanilla protein powder
¼ cup pumpkin seeds
½ cup seedless
    strawberry jam

1. Line an 8-inch square baking dish with parchment paper.

2. In a medium bowl, mix together the peanut butter, maple syrup, and vanilla until blended. Add the oats, protein powder, and pumpkin seeds and mix until well combined. If the mixture seems too sticky, add some more oats.

3. Press the mixture firmly into the prepared baking dish. If it is sticky, place a piece of parchment on the surface before pressing. Spread the jam in a thin layer over the top.

4. Place the baking dish in the freezer until it is set, about 1 hour.

5. Cut into 10 bars and serve. Store leftovers in a sealed container in the freezer for up to 1 month.

TIP: For a decadent treat, drizzle melted dark chocolate on the bars once they are frozen, about 2 ounces will be perfect. Don't like peanut butter or have an allergy? Omit it and use almond butter or cashew butter instead.

Per serving (1 bar): Calories: 278; Protein: 10g; Carbohydrates: 27g; Fiber: 2.5g; Total fat: 16g; Saturated fat: 3g; Sugar: 17g; Sodium: 112mg

Chocolate-Coconut Protein Truffles

These high-protein, low-sugar truffles are decadent. Dairy- and gluten-free, they balance sweetness with nuttiness. Dark chocolate gives the truffles flavor depth. Use a chocolate protein powder or go for a peanut butter–flavored protein powder.

DAIRY-FREE   VEGAN
GLUTEN-FREE

Prep time: 20 minutes, plus 45 minutes to chill
Makes 20 truffles

1 cup unsweetened shredded coconut, divided
½ cup natural almond butter
¼ cup gluten-free rolled oats
¼ cup almond flour
¼ cup ground flaxseed
2 scoops unsweetened chocolate protein powder
2 tablespoons unsweetened cocoa powder
2 tablespoons maple syrup
1 teaspoon pure vanilla extract

1. In a blender, combine ½ cup of coconut, the almond butter, oats, almond flour, ground flaxseed, protein powder, cocoa powder, maple syrup, and vanilla and pulse until the mixture is a well combined paste.

2. Gather the dough into a ball, cover with plastic wrap, and refrigerate for 15 minutes, or until it is firm enough to roll into individual balls.

3. Place the remaining ½ cup of coconut in a small bowl. Roll the dough into 20 balls (a little smaller than a golf ball), then roll each ball in the coconut.

4. Arrange the truffles on a baking sheet and transfer to the freezer. Freeze for about 30 minutes, or until very firm.

5. Serve immediately or transfer to a sealed container and freeze for up to 2 months.

TIP: These truffles are perfect for meal prepping, so make a large batch and stash them in the freezer for the week ahead. Grab two, and you're out the door.

Per serving (2 truffles): Calories: 200; Protein: 8g; Carbohydrates: 11g; Fiber: 4.5g; Total fat: 14g; Saturated fat: 5g; Sugar: 4g; Sodium: 51mg

Brussels Sprouts with Cumin and Sunflower Seeds

Brussels sprouts are high in fiber, protein, and calcium, so they'll help fill you up and strengthen your bones and muscles. This take on a side slaw or salad pairs well with grilled or roasted chicken breast and with salmon fillets. For extra fats and protein, top the Brussels sprouts with pistachios or slivered almonds instead of sunflower seeds.

ALLERGEN-FREE NUT-FREE
DAIRY-FREE VEGAN
GLUTEN-FREE

Prep time: 10 minutes
Cook time: 20 minutes
Serves 4

1 pound Brussels
   sprouts, halved
1 tablespoon olive oil
¼ teaspoon ground cumin
Sea salt
Juice of 1 lime
¼ cup roasted
   sunflower seeds

1. Preheat the oven to 400°F. Line a baking sheet with parchment paper.

2. In a large bowl, toss together the Brussels sprouts, oil, cumin, and salt to taste until well coated. Spread the Brussels sprouts in a single layer on the prepared baking sheet.

3. Bake for 10 minutes. Stir the sprouts and continue to bake for another 10 minutes, or until lightly caramelized and tender.

4. Transfer the sprouts to a serving bowl, toss with the lime juice, and serve topped with sunflower seeds. Store leftovers in a sealed container in the refrigerator for up to 3 days.

TIP: Add some crumbled goat cheese or feta cheese. Shaved Parmesan would also work well.

Per serving: Calories: 122; Protein: 5g; Carbohydrates: 12g; Fiber: 4.5g; Total fat: 7.5g; Saturated fat: 1g; Sugar: 2.5g; Sodium: 117mg

Spaghetti Squash with Roasted Garlic and Feta ⊛◯

Spaghetti squash allows you to enjoy "pasta" night without so many simple carbs. This bright, savory dish is high in beta-carotene, an antioxidant promoting heart health, and has fiber for satiety.

GLUTEN-FREE **VEGETARIAN** **NUT-FREE**

Prep time: 10 minutes
Cook time: 30 minutes
Serves 4

1 spaghetti squash, halved and seeded
1½ teaspoons olive oil, divided
4 garlic cloves, peeled
Freshly ground black pepper
½ cup crumbled feta cheese
¼ cup roasted pumpkin seeds

1. Preheat the oven to 400°F. Line a baking sheet with parchment paper.

2. Rub the cut halves of the squash with 1 teaspoon of oil and place them cut-side down on the prepared baking sheet. Use a fork to pierce the halves through the skin several times. Toss the garlic cloves in the remaining ½ teaspoon of oil and place them on the baking sheet with the squash.

3. Bake for 30 minutes, or until the squash is fork-tender but still a little firm. Let cool for 10 minutes, then use a fork to shred the flesh into a serving bowl.

4. Mash the roasted garlic into a creamy paste, toss it with the spaghetti squash, and season with pepper.

5. Serve topped with the feta and pumpkin seeds. Store leftovers in a sealed container in the refrigerator for up to 3 days.

TIP: To make it easier to cut the squash, microwave it whole for 30 seconds to 1 minute to soften the outside, so the knife doesn't slip off and create a cutting hazard.

Per serving: Calories: 234; Protein: 8g; Carbohydrates: 30g; Fiber: 6.5g; Total fat: 12g; Saturated fat: 4g; Sugar: 12g; Sodium: 257mg

Dijon Mustard Green Beans ⊛⚡

These green beans get a Dijon mustard and black pepper kick balanced by the acidity of lime. If you don't like green beans, try asparagus, which provides a similar texture and nutritional profile. Broccoli or snap peas would also make good substitutes. Go with what's in season—buying and cooking seasonally means using whole foods at their peak of freshness.

ALLERGEN-FREE **NUT-FREE**
DAIRY-FREE **VEGAN**
GLUTEN-FREE

Prep time: 15 minutes
Cook time: 10 minutes
Serves 4

1 pound green
   beans, trimmed
1 tablespoon
   Dijon mustard
Juice of 1 lime
Freshly ground
   black pepper

1. Fill a medium saucepan three-quarters with water and bring to a boil over high heat. Add the green beans and boil until tender-crisp, about 2 minutes. Drain.

2. Meanwhile, in a small bowl, stir together the mustard and lime juice.

3. Add the mustard mixture to the beans and toss to coat. Season with pepper and serve. Store leftovers in a sealed container in the refrigerator for up to 3 days.

Per serving: Calories: 36; Protein: 2g; Carbohydrates: 7g; Fiber: 2.5g; Total fat: 0g; Saturated fat: 0g; Sugar: 3.5g; Sodium: 96mg

Curry Sweet Potato Fries ✸

You can enjoy the salty taste and crispiness of French fries with this recipe, which calls for antioxidant-rich sweet potatoes, but you can use white potatoes, if you prefer. Curry powder has anti-inflammatory properties to promote disease prevention, muscle relaxation, and brain and heart health. Feel free to vary the size of the potato strips to make thicker or thinner fries.

ALLERGEN-FREE **NUT-FREE**
DAIRY-FREE **VEGAN**
GLUTEN-FREE

Prep time: 15 minutes, plus 30 minutes to soak
Cook time: 30 minutes
Serves 2

2 sweet potatoes, peeled and cut into ¼-inch-thick strips
1 tablespoon olive oil
1 tablespoon cornstarch
1 teaspoon curry powder
¼ teaspoon garlic powder
¼ teaspoon sea salt

1. Place the sweet potatoes in a large bowl filled with cold water and let stand for 30 minutes. Drain and pat dry the potatoes and bowl thoroughly with paper towels or a kitchen towel.

2. Preheat the oven to 400°F. Line a baking sheet with parchment paper.

3. Return the sweet potatoes to the bowl, add the oil, and toss until coated.

4. In a small bowl, stir together the cornstarch, curry powder, garlic powder, and salt until well blended. Add the mixture to the sweet potatoes and toss with your hands until thoroughly coated. Spread the potatoes in a single layer on the prepared baking sheet.

5. Bake for 15 minutes. Turn the fries and continue to bake for another 15 minutes, or until crispy and golden. Serve immediately.

TIP: Instead of spiced fries, go for something more herbaceous: Use herbs like rosemary or thyme and include some garlic—and serve with a yogurt-based sauce. Or for a sweeter batch of fries, use cinnamon, vanilla, and a hint of brown sugar or maple syrup.

Per serving: Calories: 187; Protein: 2g; Carbohydrates: 30g; Fiber: 4g; Total fat: 7g; Saturated fat: 1g; Sugar: 5.5g; Sodium: 363mg

Pesto Cauliflower "Steaks" ⚙️◻️⚡

Cauliflower is a great stand-in for steak (yes, it's true!) because it has a "meaty" texture. And cauliflower is lower in carbs, calories, and fat—win-win!

GLUTEN-FREE **VEGETARIAN**

Prep time: 10 minutes
Cook time: 20 minutes
Serves 4

---

1 large head cauliflower, cut into 4 "steaks" (see Tip) about ½ inch thick
4 tablespoons Classic Basil Pesto (page 127) or store-bought
½ cup shredded Asiago cheese
2 tablespoons pine nuts

1. Preheat the oven to 400°F. Line a baking sheet with parchment paper.

2. Place the cauliflower steaks on the prepared baking sheet in a single layer and top each with 1 tablespoon of pesto, spreading it evenly. Sprinkle 2 tablespoons of Asiago and 1½ teaspoons of pine nuts over each steak.

3. Bake for 20 minutes, or until the cheese is melted and the edges are golden. Serve warm.

TIP: Set the head of cauliflower on a cutting board stem-side up. Cutting through the core of the cauliflower (so the pieces will hold together), slice vertically all the way through to cut into "steaks" about ½ inch thick. (Save the scraps of cauliflower for another use.)

Per serving: Calories: 198; Protein: 8g; Carbohydrates: 10g; Fiber: 3g; Total fat: 15g; Saturated fat: 3.5g; Sugar: 3g; Sodium: 301mg

Lemon Herb Pilaf ⊖

Bulgar is naturally gluten-free and has more fiber and protein than the white rice traditionally used in pilafs. This pilaf works nicely as a savory side dish or as a base for a grain, protein, or egg bowl, and could even be a filling for breakfast burritos or an addition to chicken noodle soup or a plant-based chili. This pilaf is ideal for meal prep because it stores well.

ALLERGEN-FREE **NUT-FREE**
DAIRY-FREE **VEGAN**
GLUTEN-FREE

Prep time: 10 minutes
Cook time: 30 minutes
Serves 4

2 teaspoons olive oil
½ small sweet
   onion, chopped
2 teaspoons minced garlic
2 cups Low-Sodium Vege-
   table Broth (page 120)
   or store-bought
1 cup bulgur
Grated zest of 1 lemon
Juice of 1 lemon
2 teaspoons chopped
   fresh thyme or
   1 teaspoon dried
1 teaspoon chopped
   fresh basil or
   ½ teaspoon dried
1 teaspoon chopped
   fresh oregano or
   ½ teaspoon dried
Sea salt
Freshly ground
   black pepper

1. In a large saucepan, heat the oil over medium-high heat. Add the onion and garlic and sauté for about 3 minutes, or until softened.

2. Add the broth and bulgur, stir, and bring to a boil. Reduce the heat to low, partially cover the pan, and simmer for about 20 minutes, or until the bulgur is very tender.

3. Fluff the bulgur with a fork and stir in the lemon zest, lemon juice, thyme, basil, and oregano. Season lightly with salt and pepper and serve. Store leftovers in a sealed container in the refrigerator for up to 3 days.

TIP: Brown rice, quinoa, farro, and wheat berries all make lovely pilafs. If you'd prefer to use another grain here, substitute it in the same amount as the bulgur and adjust the cooking time as needed.

Per serving: Calories: 164; Protein: 5g; Carbohydrates: 32g; Fiber: 5.5g; Total fat: 2.5g; Saturated fat: 0.5g; Sugar: 3g; Sodium: 117mg

Tofu Mango Bowls, page 65

Chapter Five

PLANT-BASED MAINS

Kale Sweet Potato Chickpea Salad

Kale is a sturdy leafy green that offers iron and protein, and is a great base for a salad combined with antioxidant-rich sweet potatoes and fiber-dense chickpeas. If you like spice, definitely include the jalapeño pepper.

GLUTEN-FREE **VEGETARIAN**
NUT-FREE

Prep time: 15 minutes
Cook time: 30 minutes
Serves 4

2 sweet potatoes,
    peeled and cut into
    1-inch chunks
1 tablespoon olive oil
Sea salt
Freshly ground
    black pepper
6 cups shredded
    kale (stemmed and
    deribbed), thoroughly
    washed and dried
1 (15-ounce) can no-salt-
    added chickpeas,
    drained and rinsed
1 red bell pepper, chopped
¼ red onion, chopped
½ jalapeño pepper,
    seeded and finely
    chopped (optional)
½ cup Avocado Yogurt
    Dressing (page 126) or
    store-bought

1. Preheat the oven to 425°F. Line a baking sheet with parchment paper.

2. Spread the sweet potatoes on the prepared baking sheet, drizzle with the oil, and season lightly with salt and pepper.

3. Roast for 15 minutes. Toss the potatoes and continue to roast for another 15 minutes, or until tender and lightly caramelized.

4. Let the sweet potatoes cool to room temperature.

5. In a large bowl, toss together the kale, sweet potatoes, chickpeas, bell pepper, onion, and jalapeño (if using) until well combined.

6. Serve drizzled generously with the dressing. Store leftovers of salad and dressing in separate sealed containers in the refrigerator for up to 5 days.

TIP: You're cooking the sweet potatoes from scratch here, but you can meal prep earlier in the week and cook them ahead of time, which will cut down on kitchen time drastically, making it an even quicker to put together your meal.

Per serving: Calories: 245; Protein: 8g; Carbohydrates: 35g; Fiber: 9g; Total fat: 9g; Saturated fat: 1g; Sugar: 7g; Sodium: 145mg

Tofu Mango Bowls ⚡

If you follow a plant-based lifestyle and don't eat animal protein, you should include protein-rich tofu in your diet. This tofu bowl balances sweet and savory by combining vitamin C–rich mango with antioxidant-rich carrot, bok choy, avocado, and cilantro. Try drizzling some Thai-Inspired Peanut Sauce (page 125) on top.

DAIRY-FREE **VEGAN**
GLUTEN-FREE

Prep time: 20 minutes
Cook time: 10 minutes
Serves 2

7 ounces extra-firm tofu,
   cut into ½-inch cubes
Juice of 1 lemon
½ teaspoon ground
   coriander
1 teaspoon sesame oil
2 cups chopped bok choy
1 avocado, peeled,
   pitted, and cut into
   ½-inch chunks
1 mango, peeled,
   pitted, and cut into
   ½-inch chunks
1 large carrot, shredded
1 scallion, thinly sliced on
   the diagonal
1 tablespoon chopped
   fresh cilantro
¼ cup chopped cashews

1. In a small bowl, toss together the tofu, lemon juice, and coriander.

2. In a medium skillet, heat the oil over high heat. Add the tofu and sauté for about 5 minutes, or until crispy and golden on all sides. Add the bok choy and sauté for 2 minutes.

3. Divide the tofu and bok choy between two bowls. Arrange the avocado, mango, carrot, and scallion in each bowl and serve topped with the cilantro and cashews. Store leftovers of the tofu mixture and the individual toppings in separate containers in the refrigerator for up to 5 days.

TIP: If you can't find fresh, ripe mango, it's fine to use frozen. Thaw the mango in the refrigerator overnight to retain its texture.

Per serving: Calories: 439; Protein: 17g; Carbohydrates: 45g; Fiber: 11g; Total fat: 25g; Saturated fat: 3.5g; Sugar: 27g; Sodium: 85mg

Shredded Brussels Sprout Salad with Goat Cheese ⊛⚡

Brussels sprouts taste great roasted or as crispy chips, but you may not know that they can also be enjoyed raw. Simply shred the sprouts very thinly and toss them with nuts, cheese, and a bit of olive oil or an herbaceous dressing. Amazing, right?

GLUTEN-FREE **VEGETARIAN**

Prep time: 25 minutes
Serves 4

2 pounds Brussels sprouts,
  shredded
2 scallions, chopped
½ cup Citrus Thyme
  Dressing (page 122) or
  store-bought
½ cup crumbled soft
  goat cheese
¼ cup chopped pistachios

1. In a large bowl, toss together the Brussels sprouts, scallions, and dressing.

2. Arrange the salad on four plates and divide the goat cheese and pistachios equally among them. Serve immediately. Store the dressed salad and the individual toppings in the refrigerator in separate sealed containers for up to 3 days.

TIP: Instead of the Citrus Thyme Dressing, go with the Avocado Yogurt Dressing (page 126), which adds a creamier, thicker texture that complements both the goat cheese and pistachios.

Per serving: Calories: 336; Protein: 11g; Carbohydrates: 22g; Fiber: 9.5g; Total fat: 25g; Saturated fat: 5.5g; Sugar: 5.5g; Sodium: 146mg

Falafel Baby Green Salad

Falafel is made from high-fiber chickpeas that are mashed and formed into balls that are usually then deep-fried, but here they are baked. You can stuff falafel inside a pita or a lettuce wrap or use them as a plant-based protein source for a main dish salad. Serve over a baby greens salad dressed with creamy Avocado Yogurt Dressing (page 126) for a light but filling dish you can enjoy for lunch or dinner.

GLUTEN-FREE **VEGETARIAN**

Prep time: 15 minutes
Cook time: 20 minutes
Serves 4

1 (15-ounce) can no-salt-added chickpeas, drained and rinsed
¼ cup almond flour
¼ cup chopped onion
1 tablespoon chopped fresh parsley
2 teaspoons minced garlic
1 teaspoon ground cumin
½ teaspoon ground coriander
Olive oil spray
6 cups mixed baby greens
1 cup halved cherry tomatoes
½ cucumber, chopped
½ cup Avocado Yogurt Dressing (page 126)
¼ cup chopped cashews
2 tablespoons chopped fresh cilantro

1. Preheat the oven to 400°F. Line a baking sheet with parchment paper.

2. In a blender, combine the chickpeas, almond flour, onion, parsley, garlic, cumin, and coriander and pulse until the ingredients stick together when pressed.

3. Form the mixture into 16 (1½-inch) balls and place them on the prepared baking sheet. Flatten the balls into patties and mist them lightly with olive oil spray.

4. Bake for 10 minutes. Turn the falafels and continue to bake for another 10 minutes, or until golden.

5. Arrange the baby greens on four plates and top with the tomatoes and cucumber. Place 2 falafel patties on each plate and drizzle each serving with 2 tablespoons of dressing. Serve topped with the cashews and cilantro. Store any leftover falafel, salad makings, and dressing in the refrigerator in separate sealed containers for up to 4 days.

TIP: If you want a bolder spice profile, top the falafel with Sriracha or hot sauce, too. In fact, a drizzle of it would complement the avocado yogurt dressing's cooling, creamy effect.

Per serving: Calories: 235; Protein: 10g; Carbohydrates: 26g; Fiber: 8.5g; Total fat: 11g; Saturated fat: 1.5g; Sugar: 4.5g; Sodium: 117mg

Middle Eastern–Inspired Red Lentil Soup ⬭

This lovely plant-based soup uses red lentils for their beautiful color and high fiber and protein content. Kefir or Greek yogurt provides a cooling element and a probiotic punch for gut and immune health.

Prep time: 10 minutes
Cook time: 40 minutes
Serves 4

1 tablespoon olive oil

1 sweet onion, chopped

2 celery stalks, chopped

1 carrot, chopped

1 tablespoon minced garlic

1 teaspoon grated peeled
    fresh ginger

6 cups Low-Sodium Vege-
    table Broth (page 120) or
    store-bought

1½ cups red lentils, rinsed
    and picked over

1 large sweet potato,
    peeled and cut into
    ½-inch chunks

2 teaspoons ground cumin

1 teaspoon ground
    coriander

2 cups baby spinach

Sea salt

Freshly ground
    black pepper

½ cup plain kefir or 0%
    plain Greek yogurt

1. In a large soup pot, heat the oil over medium-high heat. Add the onion, celery, carrot, garlic, and ginger and sauté for about 6 minutes, or until softened.

2. Stir in the broth, lentils, sweet potato, cumin, and coriander. Bring the soup to a boil, then reduce the heat to low and simmer for 25 to 30 minutes until the lentils and vegetables are very tender.

3. Stir in the spinach and simmer for 1 minute longer to wilt the greens. Season lightly with salt and pepper.

4. Spoon the soup into bowls and serve with a drizzle of kefir. Store cooled leftovers in a sealed container in the refrigerator for up to 4 days.

TIP: Feel free to omit the spinach and use another green, like kale. You can also add more green veggies, like green beans, if you like.

Per serving: Calories: 414; Protein: 22g; Carbohydrates: 72g; Fiber: 13g; Total fat: 5.5g; Saturated fat: 1g; Sugar: 12g; Sodium: 343mg

Smoky Black Bean Chili ⊜

This plant-based version of the classic comfort food has a thick texture thanks to black beans, carrot, and tomatoes. If you aren't vegan, you can top it with some shredded cheese or a spoonful of plain Greek yogurt. And if you do want some meat, ground turkey or extra-lean beef would taste great.

ALLERGEN-FREE **NUT-FREE**
DAIRY-FREE **VEGAN**
GLUTEN-FREE

Prep time: 15 minutes
Cook time: 55 minutes
Serves 4

1 tablespoon olive oil
1 onion, chopped
1 tablespoon minced garlic
1 carrot, chopped
1 green bell
  pepper, chopped
1 red bell pepper, chopped
1 (28-ounce) can no-salt-
  added diced tomatoes
1 (15-ounce) can black
  beans, drained
  and rinsed
3 tablespoons chili powder
1 teaspoon
  smoked paprika
½ teaspoon ground cumin

Optional toppings
Avocado
Shredded cheese
Sliced jalapeños
Tortilla chips
Greek yogurt
Chopped fresh cilantro

1. In a large soup pot, heat the oil over medium-high heat. Add the onion and garlic and sauté for about 4 minutes, or until softened.

2. Add the carrot, green bell pepper, and red bell pepper and sauté for 4 minutes.

3. Stir in the tomatoes with their juices, black beans, chili powder, smoked paprika, and cumin. Bring the chili to a boil, then reduce the heat to low, cover, and simmer for 45 minutes, stirring occasionally, to mellow the flavors.

4. Serve the chili with any desired toppings. Store leftover cooled chili in a sealed container in the refrigerator for up to 4 days or in the freezer for up to 1 month.

TIP: This chili can also be made in a slow cooker. Omit the olive oil and the sautéing step, throw all the other ingredients into the pot, and cook, covered, on low heat for 8 hours.

Per serving (without toppings): Calories: 194; Protein: 8g; Carbohydrates: 29g; Fiber: 8g; Total fat: 4.5g; Saturated fat: 0.5g; Sugar: 8.5g; Sodium: 64mg

Spicy Tofu Tacos

Although it can be bland on its own, tofu is a flavorful plant-based protein when infused with spices like cayenne, smoked paprika, and cumin.

GLUTEN-FREE **VEGETARIAN** **NUT-FREE**

Prep time: 20 minutes, plus 30 minutes to press the tofu
Cook time: 10 minutes
Serves 4

1 (14-ounce) block extra-firm tofu
2 tablespoons olive oil, divided
1 teaspoon chili powder
1 teaspoon ground cumin
1 teaspoon smoked paprika
1 teaspoon garlic powder
½ teaspoon onion powder
⅛ teaspoon sea salt
⅛ teaspoon cayenne pepper (optional)
8 corn taco shells

1½ cups shredded lettuce
1 cup Pico de Gallo (page 121) or store-bought
½ cup Avocado Yogurt Dressing (page 126) or 0% plain Greek yogurt
½ cup crumbled feta cheese or queso fresco
2 tablespoons chopped fresh cilantro
1 lime, cut into wedges

1. Drain the tofu, wrap it in a clean kitchen towel, and place it on a plate. Put a heavy can or book on top and press the tofu for about 30 minutes.

2. Crumble the tofu into a medium bowl. Add 1 tablespoon of oil, the chili powder, cumin, paprika, garlic powder, onion powder, salt, and cayenne (if using) and toss to combine.

3. In a large skillet, heat the remaining 1 tablespoon of oil over medium-high heat. Add the tofu and sauté for about 10 minutes, or until slightly crispy, golden, and dry.

4. Divide the tofu equally among the taco shells and top with lettuce, pico de gallo, dressing, feta, and cilantro. Serve with lime wedges for squeezing. Store leftover taco components separately in sealed containers in the refrigerator for up to 4 days.

TIP: For a nuttier, kind of spicy taco, swap in Thai-Inspired Peanut Sauce (page 125) and omit the pico de gallo and dressing.

Per serving (2 tacos): Calories: 402; Protein: 16g; Carbohydrates: 27g; Fiber: 5.5g; Total fat: 26g; Saturated fat: 7g; Sugar: 5g; Sodium: 486mg

Classic Ratatouille with Fresh Mozzarella ⊖

Ratatouille is high in both fiber and antioxidants that are good for your skin as well as your heart and digestive health. Serve the ratatouille over cooked rice, quinoa, or whole-grain pasta.

GLUTEN-FREE **VEGETARIAN**
NUT-FREE

Prep time: 15 minutes
Cook time: 50 minutes
Serves 4

1 tablespoon olive oil
½ sweet onion, chopped
1 tablespoon minced garlic
½ small eggplant,
   peeled and cut into
   1-inch chunks
2 zucchini, cut into
   ½-inch chunks
1 yellow bell pepper, cut
   into ½-inch chunks
1 red bell pepper, cut into
   ½-inch chunks

1 (28-ounce) can no-salt-
   added diced tomatoes
1 tablespoon dried basil
1 teaspoon dried oregano
Pinch red pepper flakes
2 cups shredded kale
   (stemmed and deribbed)
Sea salt
Freshly ground
   black pepper
2 ounces fresh mozzarella
   cheese, shredded

1. In a large soup pot, heat the oil over medium-high heat. Add the onion and garlic and sauté for about 3 minutes, or until softened.

2. Add the eggplant, zucchini, yellow bell pepper, red bell pepper, tomatoes with their juices, basil, oregano, and red pepper flakes. Bring to a high simmer, then reduce the heat to low and cook, stirring occasionally, for about 45 minutes, or until the vegetables are very tender and the stew is thick. Season lightly with salt and black pepper.

3. Serve topped with the mozzarella. Store the ratatouille and mozzarella in separate sealed containers in the refrigerator for up to 4 days.

Per serving: Calories: 198; Protein: 8g; Carbohydrates: 29g; Fiber: 7g; Total fat: 6.5g; Saturated fat: 2g; Sugar: 15g; Sodium: 138mg

Veggie Bean Sprout Chow Mein ⊝

Take-out chow mein is often a very salty, carbohydrate-dense, and less-than-healthy meal. This version gets a makeover by ditching the noodles for veggies. It is scented with heart-healthy fresh garlic and ginger.

DAIRY-FREE **NUT-FREE**
GLUTEN-FREE **VEGAN**

Prep time: 20 minutes
Cook time: 15 minutes
Serves 2

1 tablespoon sesame
   oil, divided
1 tablespoon minced garlic
1 tablespoon grated
   peeled fresh ginger
2 cups small broccoli
   florets
1 red bell pepper,
   thinly sliced
1 cup slivered bok choy
1 cup shredded carrot
1 cup halved snow peas
2 cups bean sprouts
2 tablespoons
   reduced-sodium tamari
1 scallion, chopped
1 tablespoon
   sesame seeds

1. In a large skillet, heat the oil over medium-high heat. Add the garlic and ginger and sauté for about 2 minutes, or until fragrant.

2. Add the broccoli, bell pepper, bok choy, and carrot and sauté for about 7 minutes, or until tender-crisp.

3. Add the snow peas, bean sprouts, tamari, and scallion and sauté for 3 minutes.

4. Divide between two plates and serve topped with the sesame seeds. Store leftovers in a sealed container in the refrigerator for up to 4 days.

TIP: Bean sprouts can be hard to find, and even when they are available, they can look past their prime. If you can't get good bean sprouts, try spiralized zucchini instead, which can be found in the produce section of most grocery stores.

Per serving: Calories: 216; Protein: 11g; Carbohydrates: 24g; Fiber: 7g; Total fat: 10g; Saturated fat: 1.5g; Sugar: 11g; Sodium: 775mg

Acorn Squash Stuffed with Bulgur, Grapes, and Walnuts

Squash is rich in fiber and beta-carotene, an antioxidant that promotes heart health. Walnuts add anti-inflammatory omega-3 fats to boost cognitive health, and bulgur adds fiber. The seedless grapes and celery provide sweetness and crunch.

DAIRY-FREE   **VEGAN**

Prep time: 15 minutes
Cook time: 1 hour
Serves 2

1 medium acorn squash,
   halved and seeded
1 cup water
½ cup bulgur
1 cup halved seedless
   red grapes
½ cup chopped walnuts
1 celery stalk,
   finely chopped
Grated zest of 1 lemon
2 teaspoons chopped
   fresh thyme
Sea salt
Freshly ground
   black pepper

1. Preheat the oven to 400°F. Line a baking sheet with parchment paper.

2. Place the squash halves cut-side up on the prepared baking sheet. Bake for 50 minutes, or until tender. Let cool for 10 minutes. (Leave the oven on.)

3. Meanwhile, in a medium saucepan, combine the water and bulgur and bring to a boil over high heat. Reduce the heat to low and simmer for about 25 minutes, or until the bulgur is tender and the liquid is absorbed.

4. In a medium bowl, combine the bulgur, grapes, walnuts, celery, lemon zest, and thyme. Season lightly with salt and pepper.

5. Divide the filling between the squash halves, return to the oven, and bake for 10 minutes to heat through.

6. Serve immediately. Store leftovers in a sealed container in the refrigerator for up to 4 days.

TIP: Almost any squash is an excellent container for this filling, even summer squash. Try butternut or zucchini with the flesh scooped out to create a hollow. You can also use tomatoes or bell peppers as a container for the filling.

Per serving: Calories: 471; Protein: 11g; Carbohydrates: 69g; Fiber: 11g; Total fat: 20g; Saturated fat: 2g; Sugar: 18g; Sodium: 107mg

Penne Primavera ⚡

Whole-grain penne is a healthier alternative to pasta made with refined flour. Mushrooms, bell pepper, and green beans add fiber and minerals for fuel. If you like heat, be sure to season this primavera with red pepper flakes. They might give your metabolism a little boost!

NUT-FREE　**VEGETARIAN**

Prep time: 15 minutes
Cook time: 15 minutes
Serves 2

4 ounces whole-grain
　penne
1 teaspoon olive oil
1 cup sliced mushrooms
½ sweet onion, chopped
2 teaspoons minced garlic
1 yellow bell pepper, cut
　into thin strips
1 cup (1-inch pieces)
　green beans
1 cup halved cherry
　tomatoes
¼ cup Low-Sodium Vege-
　table Broth (page 120) or
　store-bought
Grated zest of ½ lemon
Juice of ½ lemon
2 tablespoons grated
　Parmesan cheese
1 tablespoon chopped
　fresh basil
Pinch red pepper flakes
　(optional)
Sea salt
Freshly ground
　black pepper

1. Fill a large saucepan three-quarters with water and bring to a boil over high heat. Add the pasta and cook to al dente according to the package directions. Drain and set aside.

2. Meanwhile, in a large skillet, heat the oil over medium-high heat. Add the mushrooms, onion, and garlic and sauté for about 5 minutes, or until softened.

3. Add the bell pepper and green beans and sauté for 2 minutes. Add the cherry tomatoes, broth, lemon zest, lemon juice, Parmesan, basil, and red pepper flakes (if using) and toss until combined.

4. Add the pasta to the skillet and toss to combine. Season lightly with salt and black pepper and serve. Store leftovers in a sealed container in the refrigerator for up to 4 days.

TIP: Nearly any veggie in your refrigerator can be thrown into this simple, delicious dish. Try zucchini, cauliflower, broccoli, spinach, carrots, or peas for a different look and flavor.

Per serving: Calories: 323; Protein: 15g; Carbohydrates: 63g; Fiber: 9.5g; Total fat: 6g; Saturated fat: 1g; Sugar: 14g; Sodium: 203mg

Chickpea Curry ⊜

Chickpeas and brown rice make this Indian-inspired curry a protein- and fiber-rich dinner option. The combination of cumin, curry, and ginger offers anti-inflammatory benefits and gives this dish a bold flavor profile. Serve the curry with rice or pita, spoon it over greens, or use it in a lettuce wrap. If you eat meat, you can add diced chicken for a protein boost.

ALLERGEN-FREE **NUT-FREE**
DAIRY-FREE **VEGAN**
GLUTEN-FREE

Prep time: 10 minutes
Cook time: 25 minutes
Serves 4

2 teaspoons olive oil

½ sweet onion, chopped

2 teaspoons minced garlic

2 teaspoons grated peeled fresh ginger

2 tablespoons curry powder

1 teaspoon ground cumin

½ teaspoon ground coriander

2 (15-ounce) cans no-salt-added chickpeas, drained and rinsed

1 (15-ounce) can no-salt-added diced tomatoes

2 tablespoons chopped fresh cilantro

1. In a large saucepan, heat the oil over medium-high heat. Add the onion, garlic, and ginger and sauté for about 4 minutes, or until softened.

2. Add the curry, cumin, and coriander and sauté for about 1 minute, or until fragrant. Add the chickpeas and tomatoes with their juices and bring to a gentle boil. Reduce the heat to low and simmer for 20 minutes to mellow the flavors and thicken the curry slightly.

3. Serve garnished with the cilantro. Store leftovers in a sealed container in the refrigerator for up to 4 days.

TIP: Using Thai curry paste is an option instead of Indian-style curry powder. The paste can add a richer flavor, and you can choose among three types of curry paste: red, yellow, and green.

Per serving: Calories: 240; Protein: 10g; Carbohydrates: 38g; Fiber: 10g; Total fat: 5.5g; Saturated fat: 0.5g; Sugar: 7.5g; Sodium: 39mg

Lentil Brown Rice Veggie Burgers

Veggie burgers can taste just as delicious as beef or turkey burgers, and they help lower your saturated fat intake to improve your heart health and reduce your cholesterol levels. Lentils and brown rice provide plenty of fiber and protein.

DAIRY-FREE **VEGAN**
GLUTEN-FREE

Prep time: 10 minutes, plus 15 minutes to chill
Cook time: 10 minutes
Serves 4

½ cup cooked brown rice
1 (15-ounce) can no-salt-added lentils, drained and rinsed
½ cup almonds
½ sweet onion, finely chopped
½ cup shredded carrot
2 parsley sprigs
2 teaspoons minced garlic
1 teaspoon ground cumin
Sea salt
Freshly ground black pepper
Olive oil spray
4 large lettuce leaves
Favorite burger toppings

1. Place the cooked rice into a blender and add the lentils, almonds, onion, carrot, parsley, garlic, and cumin. Pulse until the ingredients are finely chopped and stick together when pressed.

2. Transfer the mixture to a bowl, season lightly with salt and pepper, and divide into 4 equal portions. Form into patties and refrigerate for at least 15 minutes.

3. Position a rack in the top third of the oven and preheat the oven to broil. Line a baking sheet with aluminum foil.

4. Place the chilled patties on the prepared baking sheet and mist both sides of the patties with olive oil spray.

5. Broil the burgers for 5 minutes. Flip the burgers and broil for about 5 more minutes, or until the patties are golden and heated through.

6. Serve each burger on a lettuce leaf with your favorite toppings.

7. Store leftover burgers in a sealed container in the refrigerator for up to 4 days.

TIP: For a California-inspired meal, try these burgers topped with sliced tomato, avocado, and Tzatziki Sauce (page 123) or Avocado Yogurt Dressing (page 126).

Per serving (without toppings): Calories: 306; Protein: 14g; Carbohydrates: 43g; Fiber: 12g; Total fat: 10g; Saturated fat: 1g; Sugar: 5.5g; Sodium: 376mg

Baja Halibut Tacos with Lime, page 81

Chapter Six

FISH AND SHELLFISH

Spinach Grapefruit Salad with Broiled Shrimp ⚡

This light, fruity salad gets a burst of citrus from fresh grapefruit and is topped with an herbaceous dressing. If ruby red grapefruit is too tart for you, try pink or white grapefruit or use orange slices. Edamame is an excellent plant-based protein that will help keep you satiated.

DAIRY-FREE **NUT-FREE**
GLUTEN-FREE

Prep time: 20 minutes
Cook time: 5 minutes
Serves 2

8 ounces large shrimp,
   peeled and deveined
1 tablespoon olive oil
Sea salt
Freshly ground
   black pepper
4 cups baby spinach
¼ cup Citrus Thyme
   Dressing (page 122)
   or store-bought
1 large ruby red grapefruit,
   cut into suprêmes
   (see Tip)
½ cup frozen shelled
   edamame, thawed
1 scallion, chopped

1. Position a rack in the top third of the oven and preheat the oven to broil. Line a baking sheet with aluminum foil.

2. Arrange the shrimp on the prepared baking sheet, drizzle with the oil, and toss until coated. Season lightly with salt and pepper.

3. Broil the shrimp for 1 minute. Flip the shrimp and broil for 1 to 2 more minutes until just cooked through and pink.

4. In a large bowl, toss the spinach with half of the dressing until well mixed.

5. Evenly divide the greens between two plates and top each with half the shrimp, grapefruit segments, edamame, and scallion. Drizzle the remaining dressing over the salads and serve.

6. For best storage, dress only the amount of spinach you will be eating right away. Store all the salad components in separate sealed containers in the refrigerator for up to 3 days.

TIP: To create grapefruit segments, cut off all the skin and pith down to the flesh, then cut out the individual sections between the membranes.

Per serving: Calories: 422; Protein: 20g; Carbohydrates: 25g; Fiber: 8g; Total fat: 27g; Saturated fat: 4g; Sugar: 11g; Sodium: 681mg

Baja Halibut Tacos with Lime ⚡

These easy-to-make tacos substitute lettuce for tortillas and protein-rich halibut for red meat. Their spiciness is nicely balanced by creamy Avocado Yogurt Dressing (page 126). Cabbage adds crunch.

GLUTEN-FREE   **NUT-FREE**

Prep time: 20 minutes
Cook time: 10 minutes
Serves 2

1 teaspoon olive oil
8 ounces halibut fillets
½ teaspoon
   smoked paprika
Juice of 1 lime
¼ cup Avocado Yogurt
   Dressing (page 126)
1 teaspoon Sriracha sauce
4 large butter
   lettuce leaves
½ cup finely shredded
   red cabbage
1 tomato, chopped
1 tablespoon chopped
   fresh cilantro

1. In a medium skillet, heat the oil over medium-high heat. Season the fish on all sides with the smoked paprika, add it to the skillet, and cook for about 4 minutes per side, or until it is opaque. Transfer the halibut to a plate and, using a fork, break it up into large chunks. Drizzle the lime juice over the fish and set aside.

2. In a small bowl, stir together the dressing and Sriracha sauce until well blended.

3. Place the lettuce leaves on a clean work surface and divide the fish equally among them. Top with the cabbage, tomato, and the dressing-Sriracha mixture.

4. Serve topped with the chopped cilantro. Store leftover fish and the other taco components in separate sealed containers in the refrigerator for up to 3 days.

TIP: You can make the tacos with soft corn or flour tortillas or hard taco shells if you prefer.

Per serving (2 tacos): Calories: 159; Protein: 20g; Carbohydrates: 2g; Fiber: 1g; Total fat: 7.5g; Saturated fat: 1g; Sugar: 0.5g; Sodium: 122mg

Crab Cakes with Blood Orange Salsa

These citrusy and light crab cakes are packed with protein and healthy fats. If you have leftover crab cakes, try them over a base of greens, scrambled eggs, or brown rice.

DAIRY-FREE **GLUTEN-FREE**

Prep time: 15 minutes, plus 1 hour to chill
Cook time: 10 minutes
Serves 4

For the crab cakes

1 pound lump crabmeat, drained and picked over for shells
½ red bell pepper, finely chopped
1 scallion, chopped
¼ cup almond flour, plus more as needed
1 large egg
2 teaspoons chopped fresh parsley
1 teaspoon Dijon mustard
1 teaspoon grated lemon zest
Pinch cayenne pepper
1 tablespoon olive oil

For the salsa

2 blood oranges, peeled and chopped
1 scallion, chopped
Grated zest of ½ lime
Juice of ½ lime
1 tablespoon chopped fresh cilantro
Sea salt
Freshly ground black pepper

To make the crab cakes

1. In a medium bowl, mix together the crabmeat, bell pepper, scallion, almond flour, egg, parsley, mustard, lemon zest, and cayenne until well combined and it holds together when pressed. If not, add more almond flour.

2. Divide the crab mixture into 8 equal portions and form into patties about 1 inch thick. Arrange them on a baking sheet, cover, and refrigerate for 1 hour, or until firm.

3. In a large skillet, heat the oil over medium heat. Cook the crab cakes for 2 minutes. Flip the crab cakes and continue to cook for about 2 more minutes, or until they are golden.

To make the salsa

4. While the crab patties are chilling, in a small bowl, stir together the oranges, scallion, lime zest, lime juice, and cilantro. Season lightly with salt and pepper and refrigerate until ready to serve.

5. Set 2 crab cakes on each of four plates, top with the salsa, and serve.

TIP: The salsa and uncooked crab cakes can be made up to 3 days ahead and refrigerated in separate sealed containers until you are ready to use them.

Per serving: Calories: 207; Protein: 22g; Carbohydrates: 10g; Fiber: 2.5g; Total fat: 9g; Saturated fat: 1g; Sugar: 7g; Sodium: 615mg

Sesame Salmon Burgers ⚡

Burgers are a staple of outdoor grilling, and they're a nice protein to keep in your refrigerator or freezer. These salmon burgers have less saturated fat than a typical beef patty. Their flavor flair comes from sesame seeds, scallion, and coconut aminos.

DAIRY-FREE **GLUTEN-FREE**

Prep time: 10 minutes
Cook time: 15 minutes
Serves 2

Olive oil spray
2 (4-ounce) cans
  water-packed
  salmon, drained
1 large egg
¼ cup almond flour
  or whole wheat
  bread crumbs
1 scallion, chopped
Juice of ½ lime
¼ cup shredded carrot
¼ red bell pepper, minced
2 tablespoons
  sesame seeds
1 teaspoon coconut aminos
½ teaspoon minced garlic
¼ teaspoon grated peeled
  fresh ginger
2 large lettuce leaves
2 small whole-grain pita
  breads (optional)

1. Preheat the oven to 400°F. Line a baking sheet with parchment paper and lightly mist the parchment with olive oil spray.

2. In a medium bowl, mix together the salmon, egg, almond flour, scallion, lime juice, carrot, bell pepper, sesame seeds, coconut aminos, garlic, and ginger until well mixed. Divide the mixture into 4 equal portions and form into patties. Place them on the prepared baking sheet.

3. Bake, turning halfway through, for 15 minutes, or until browned and firm.

4. Serve on lettuce leaves. Or if desired, tuck the lettuce and the burger into a pita.

TIP: Leftover cooked salmon can be used instead of canned, or you can even use fresh salmon if you chop it into small pieces and adjust the cooking time by adding about 10 minutes.

Per serving: Calories: 335; Protein: 26g; Carbohydrates: 7g; Fiber: 3.5g; Total fat: 25g; Saturated fat: 3g; Sugar: 2.5g; Sodium: 494mg

Sheet Pan Shrimp with Vegetables ⊙⊘

Sheet pan meals are super easy to make, and this one is ready in only 30 minutes. Using shrimp and vegetables, the recipe provides lots of fiber from greens and antioxidants from bell pepper. The dressing provides a citrusy zest.

DAIRY-FREE **NUT-FREE**
GLUTEN-FREE

Prep time: 15 minutes
Cook time: 15 minutes
Serves 2

8 ounces large
  (31/35 count) shrimp,
  peeled and deveined
1 head broccoli, cut into
  small florets
12 asparagus
  spears, tough ends
  trimmed, halved
1 red bell pepper,
  thinly sliced
¼ cup Citrus Thyme
  Dressing (page 122) or
  store-bought

1. Preheat the oven to 400°F. Line a sheet pan with parchment paper.

2. Arrange the shrimp, broccoli, asparagus, and bell pepper on the prepared sheet pan. Drizzle with the dressing and toss until well coated, then spread everything out in a single layer.

3. Bake, stirring a few times, for 12 minutes, or until the shrimp are cooked through and the vegetables are tender.

4. Serve immediately. Store leftovers in a sealed container in the refrigerator for up to 3 days.

TIP: A protein plus vegetable combination can go with any starch to create a tasty balanced meal, so try this shrimp and veggie dish in a grain bowl.

Per serving: Calories: 324; Protein: 25g; Carbohydrates: 13g; Fiber: 5.5g; Total fat: 20g; Saturated fat: 3g; Sugar: 6g; Sodium: 863mg

Blackened Scallops with Wilted Balsamic Collard Greens ⚡

Scallops are high in heart-healthy fats and have a meaty texture. They taste wonderful with balsamic collard greens and some blackening spice. Even better? Scallops are easy to make in about 30 minutes. This recipe calls for the scallops to be cooked in olive oil, which provides anti-inflammatory benefits and heart-protecting unsaturated fats.

DAIRY-FREE **NUT-FREE**
GLUTEN-FREE

Prep time: 15 minutes
Cook time: 15 minutes
Serves 4

For the wilted greens
1 tablespoon olive oil
½ onion, thinly sliced
8 cups chopped collard greens (stemmed and deribbed)
1 tablespoon minced garlic
3 tablespoons balsamic vinegar
Sea salt
Freshly ground black pepper

For the scallops
1 pound sea scallops, cleaned and patted dry
3 tablespoons blackening spice
1 tablespoon olive oil

To make the wilted greens

1. In a large skillet, heat the oil over high heat. Add the onion and sauté for 2 minutes. Add the collards and garlic and, using tongs, toss for about 5 minutes, or until they are almost wilted.

2. Add the vinegar and continue tossing for about 4 minutes, or until completely wilted.

3. Remove from the heat and season lightly with salt and pepper. Set aside.

To make the scallops

4. Season the scallops all over with the blackening spice and set aside on a plate.

5. In another large skillet, heat the oil over medium-high heat. Add the scallops in a single layer so they are not touching and sear on both sides, for a total of 3 to 4 minutes.

6. Divide the collard mixture among four plates. Top with the scallops and serve.

TIP: When cleaning the scallops, make sure you remove the visible flap of tissue on the side, which is tough.

Per serving: Calories: 180; Protein: 16g; Carbohydrates: 12g; Fiber: 3g; Total fat: 7.5g; Saturated fat: 1g; Sugar: 2.5g; Sodium: 670mg

Coconut Seafood Chowder ⊖

This chowder provides heart-healthy fats and protein.

Prep time: 15 minutes
Cook time: 30 minutes
Serves 4

1 tablespoon olive oil
1 onion, chopped
1 tablespoon minced garlic
2 celery stalks, chopped
1 red bell pepper, chopped
2 cups Low-Sodium Vege-
  table Broth (page 120) or
  chicken broth
1 (14-ounce) can full-fat
  coconut milk
1 (14-ounce) can
  fire-roasted diced
  tomatoes
Juice of 1 lime

2 teaspoons ground cumin
1 teaspoon paprika
Pinch red pepper flakes
12 ounces firm, white-
  fleshed fish, cut into
  ½-inch pieces
10 large shrimp, peeled,
  deveined, and chopped
Sea salt
Freshly ground
  black pepper
¼ cup chopped fresh
  cilantro

1. In a large saucepan, heat the oil over medium-high heat. Add the onion and garlic and sauté for about 3 minutes, or until softened. Add the celery and bell pepper and sauté for 1 minute.

2. Stir in the broth, coconut milk, tomatoes with their juices, lime juice, cumin, paprika, and red pepper flakes. Bring the soup to a boil, then reduce the heat to low and simmer for 15 minutes to mellow the flavors.

3. Increase the heat to medium, add the fish and shrimp, and simmer for about 6 minutes, or until just cooked through. Season lightly with salt and black pepper.

4. Spoon into bowls and serve topped with the cilantro. Store leftovers in a sealed container in the refrigerator for up to 3 days.

TIP: Swap white fish and shrimp for lobster or crabmeat. Both complement the spices and coconut milk.

Per serving: Calories: 381; Protein: 22g; Carbohydrates: 15g; Fiber: 3.5g; Total fat: 27g; Saturated fat: 21g; Sugar: 5g; Sodium: 410mg

Mussels in Spicy Coconut Milk ⊙⚡

This silky soup gets its kick from red pepper flakes, garlic, and ginger, which together may boost your metabolic burn and provide anti-inflammation benefits. Lime adds spice-taming acidity. Try adding fresh herbs, such as basil and thyme, for aromatic notes.

DAIRY-FREE **GLUTEN-FREE**

Prep time: 15 minutes
Cook time: 15 minutes
Serves 2

1 tablespoon coconut oil
½ onion, thinly sliced
1 teaspoon minced garlic
1 teaspoon grated peeled
　fresh ginger
⅛ teaspoon red
　pepper flakes
½ cup canned full-fat
　coconut milk
½ cup low-sodium
　chicken broth
Grated zest of 1 lime
Juice of 1 lime
1½ pounds mussels,
　scrubbed and
　debearded
2 tablespoons chopped
　fresh cilantro

1. In a large skillet, heat the oil over medium-high heat. Add the onion, garlic, and ginger and sauté for about 3 minutes, or until softened. Add the red pepper flakes and toss until combined.

2. Stir in the coconut milk, broth, lime zest, and lime juice and bring to a boil. Add the mussels, cover, and steam until the shells open, about 8 minutes. Remove the skillet from the heat and discard any unopened mussels.

3. Serve immediately with the sauce and top with the cilantro.

TIP: When debearding mussels, always pull the byssal threads that protrude from the shell toward the hinge end or you will kill the mussel.

Per serving: Calories: 388; Protein: 29g; Carbohydrates: 14g; Fiber: 1.5g; Total fat: 24g; Saturated fat: 17g; Sugar: 1.5g; Sodium: 445mg

Broiled Salmon with Caponata and Pistachios ⚡

Salmon contains an abundance of omega-3 fatty acids, a type of fat that reduces inflammation in the body and can protect against heart and brain disease. Prepared with salty olives, fresh oregano and parsley, and cumin, this salmon ticks all the flavor boxes.

DAIRY-FREE   **GLUTEN-FREE**

Prep time: 15 minutes
Cook time: 15 minutes
Serves 2

3 teaspoons olive
   oil, divided
¼ onion, thinly sliced
1 teaspoon minced garlic
2 tomatoes, chopped
¼ cup chopped roasted
   red peppers
¼ cup chopped olives
2 teaspoons chopped
   fresh oregano
1 teaspoon chopped
   fresh parsley
Pinch red pepper flakes
2 (5-ounce) salmon fillets
1 teaspoon ground cumin
½ teaspoon ground
   coriander
2 tablespoons chopped
   pistachios

1. Preheat the oven to broil. Line an 8-inch baking dish with aluminum foil.

2. In a large skillet, heat 1 teaspoon of oil over medium-high heat. Add the onion and garlic and sauté for about 2 minutes, or until softened.

3. Stir in the tomatoes, roasted peppers, olives, oregano, parsley, and red pepper flakes. Reduce the heat to low and cook, stirring, for about 10 minutes to heat through.

4. Meanwhile, pat the salmon dry with paper towels and place it in the prepared baking dish. Rub the fish with the remaining 2 teaspoons of oil and season it with the cumin and coriander.

5. Broil the fish, turning once, for about 12 minutes, or until it is just cooked through.

6. Serve the fish topped with the sauce and a sprinkle of pistachios. Store leftovers of the fish and sauce in separate sealed containers in the refrigerator for up to 3 days.

TIP: If you don't like pistachios, you can use slivered almonds instead, which will still provide healthy fats, some protein, and fiber to keep you satiated.

Per serving: Calories: 395; Protein: 35g; Carbohydrates: 11g; Fiber: 3g; Total fat: 23g; Saturated fat: 3g; Sugar: 5g; Sodium: 230mg

Maple Pecan Haddock ⊛⊝⚡

Haddock is an underrated fish that happens to be super nutritious and flavorful, especially when combined with sweet maple syrup and nutty pecans. What's more, haddock is pretty low in carbs, so you can pair it with quinoa or a starch like sweet potato for gut-regulating fiber.

DAIRY-FREE **GLUTEN-FREE**

Prep time: 5 minutes
Cook time: 15 minutes
Serves 2

2 (5-ounce) skinless
   haddock fillets
Sea salt
Freshly ground
   black pepper
2 tablespoons maple syrup
2 tablespoons
   crushed pecans

1. Preheat the oven to 350°F.

2. Pat the fish dry with paper towels and season lightly on both sides with salt and pepper.

3. Place the haddock in an 8-inch square baking dish and spread the maple syrup all over the top. Sprinkle the crushed pecans on the fish.

4. Bake for 12 minutes, or until the fish is opaque and flakes when pressed with a fork. Serve immediately.

TIP: For more flavor, seek out a maple syrup with more robust flavor, such as amber or dark. And of course make sure it is a pure product and not one cut with corn syrup—read the label carefully.

Per serving: Calories: 199; Protein: 23g; Carbohydrates: 14g; Fiber: 0.5g; Total fat: 5.5g; Saturated fat: 0.5g; Sugar: 12g; Sodium: 368mg

Beef Kebabs with Garlic Marinade, page 103

Chapter Seven

MEAT AND POULTRY

Spicy Chicken Salad Lettuce Wraps ⊙⚡

Lettuce wraps can be just as delicious as sandwich wraps, but without the carbs. The chicken for this salad is tossed with a creamy dressing seasoned with cumin, cayenne, and curry powder. Curry powder has anti-inflammatory benefits to protect your heart, and cayenne pepper may give your metabolism a boost. Stuff leftovers into a whole wheat tortilla or whole-grain sandwich wrap.

GLUTEN-FREE

Prep time: 15 minutes
Serves 2

2 cups chopped cooked
  chicken breasts
  (homemade or
  store-bought rotisserie)
2 celery stalks, diced
1 scallion, thinly sliced
¼ cup 0% plain
  Greek yogurt
2 tablespoons raisins
1 teaspoon curry powder
¼ teaspoon ground cumin
⅛ teaspoon
  cayenne pepper
4 large lettuce leaves
¼ cup slivered almonds

In a medium bowl, mix together the chicken, celery, scallion, yogurt, raisins, curry powder, cumin, and cayenne until well combined. Spoon the chicken salad into the lettuce leaves, top with the almonds, and serve. Store leftovers of chicken salad and lettuce leaves in separate containers in the refrigerator for up to 4 days.

TIP: Instead of almonds, try pistachios. And you can trade heat for sweetness by omitting the curry, cumin, and cayenne and using dill, lemon juice, and some chopped grapes.

Per serving (2 wraps): Calories: 420; Protein: 60g; Carbohydrates: 14g; Fiber: 3g; Total fat: 13g; Saturated fat: 2.5g; Sugar: 8.5g; Sodium: 173mg

Lemon Chicken with Broccoli ⊖

Take-out chicken and broccoli can be high in sodium, fat, carbs, calories, MSG, and even sugar. This clean version is great for a busy weeknight dinner because it's done in only about 30 minutes. Greek yogurt provides protein and probiotics, which enhance gut health and keep you regular.

GLUTEN-FREE **NUT-FREE**

Prep time: 10 minutes
Cook time: 25 minutes
Serves 2

1 teaspoon olive oil

10 ounces boneless, skinless chicken breasts, thinly sliced

½ sweet onion, chopped

1 teaspoon grated peeled fresh ginger

½ cup low-sodium chicken broth

Grated zest of 1 lemon

Juice of 1 lemon

2 cups broccoli florets

1 teaspoon chopped fresh thyme

2 tablespoons 0% plain Greek yogurt

1. In a large skillet, heat the oil over medium-high heat. Add the chicken and sauté for about 10 minutes, or until it is just cooked through. Using a slotted spoon, transfer the chicken to a plate and set aside.

2. Add the onion and ginger to the skillet and sauté for about 3 minutes, or until softened. Add the broth, lemon zest, and lemon juice and bring to a simmer. Cook for about 5 minutes, or until the liquid is reduced by one-quarter.

3. Stir in the chicken, broccoli, and thyme and simmer for about 4 minutes, or until the broccoli is tender.

4. Stir in the yogurt and serve immediately. Store leftovers in a sealed container in the refrigerator for up to 4 days.

TIP: This dish is lovely with cooked grains, pasta, a simple baked sweet potato, or roasted vegetables.

Per serving: Calories: 250; Protein: 37g; Carbohydrates: 11g; Fiber: 2.5g; Total fat: 6.5g; Saturated fat: 1g; Sugar: 5.5g; Sodium: 113mg

Clean Chicken Cacciatore ⬭

This slimmed-down upgrade of the Italian classic gets its flavor from red pepper flakes and aromatic herbs such as thyme and oregano. Black olives add some heart-healthy unsaturated fats to boost satiety levels. Use any leftovers over zoodles or in a whole-grain tortilla.

ALLERGEN-FREE **GLUTEN-FREE**
DAIRY-FREE **NUT-FREE**

Prep time: 15 minutes
Cook time: 40 minutes
Serves 4

2 teaspoons olive oil

3 (6-ounce) boneless, skinless chicken breasts, cut into 1-inch chunks

1 cup sliced mushrooms

½ sweet onion, chopped

2 celery stalks, chopped

1 tablespoon minced garlic

1 red bell pepper, chopped

1 (28-ounce) can no-salt-added diced tomatoes

¼ cup sliced black olives

2 tablespoons tomato paste

1 teaspoon dried oregano

1 teaspoon dried thyme

⅛ teaspoon red pepper flakes

Sea salt

Freshly ground black pepper

1. In a large skillet, heat the oil over medium-high heat. Add the chicken and cook, stirring frequently, for about 5 minutes, or until browned. Using a slotted spoon, transfer the chicken to a plate and set aside.

2. Add the mushrooms, onion, celery, garlic, and bell pepper to the skillet and sauté for about 4 minutes, or until softened. Stir in the tomatoes with their juices, olives, tomato paste, oregano, thyme, and red pepper flakes. Bring to a boil. Return the chicken to the skillet, reduce the heat to low, partially cover, and simmer, stirring occasionally, for about 30 minutes, or until the chicken is tender.

3. Season lightly with salt and black pepper and serve. Store leftovers in a sealed container in the refrigerator for up to 4 days.

TIP: If you enjoy dairy in your diet, top the cacciatore with shaved Parmesan for a lovely addition.

Per serving: Calories: 257; Protein: 32g; Carbohydrates: 13g; Fiber: 3g; Total fat: 7g; Saturated fat: 1g; Sugar: 7.5g; Sodium: 413mg

Chicken Cabbage Roll Skillet ⊝

This stuffed cabbage roll comes courtesy of a super-simple skillet meal. The cabbage and Brussels sprouts are both high in fiber to fill you up, and Brussels sprouts are a good source of plant protein. Garlic may have anti-inflammatory and immunity-boosting properties. The recipe's maple syrup and balsamic vinegar balance sweetness and acidity.

ALLERGEN-FREE GLUTEN-FREE
DAIRY-FREE NUT-FREE

Prep time: 15 minutes
Cook time: 30 minutes
Serves 2

1 teaspoon olive oil
8 ounces extra-lean
   ground chicken breast
2 cups shredded cabbage
1 cup quartered
   Brussels sprouts
½ onion, chopped
2 teaspoons minced garlic
1 (15-ounce) can crushed
   tomatoes
1 tablespoon maple syrup
1 tablespoon
   balsamic vinegar
2 cups cauliflower rice

1. In large skillet, heat the oil over medium-high heat. Add the chicken and cook for about 8 minutes, or until cooked through.

2. Add the cabbage, Brussels sprouts, onion, and garlic and sauté for about 8 minutes, or until the vegetables are tender.

3. Add the tomatoes, maple syrup, and vinegar and bring to a boil. Reduce the heat to low and simmer for 10 minutes to mellow the flavors and thicken the sauce.

4. Add the cauliflower rice, cook for 2 additional minutes, and serve. Store leftovers in a sealed container in the refrigerator for up to 4 days.

TIP: Ground chicken nicely bulks up the protein, but so would lean ground beef or turkey. Both would be delicious.

Per serving: Calories: 363; Protein: 29g; Carbohydrates: 37g; Fiber: 11g; Total fat: 10g; Saturated fat: 2.5g; Sugar: 21g; Sodium: 584mg

Turkey Meatballs with Zucchini Noodles ⚡

This clean-eating version of pasta and meatballs uses low-carbohydrate and fiber-, vitamin-, and mineral-rich zucchini. Go with ground turkey breast to further reduce saturated fat and maximize protein intake. If you're short on time, buy zucchini noodles from the produce section of the store rather than making them.

DAIRY-FREE　　**GLUTEN-FREE**

Prep time: 15 minutes
Cook time: 15 minutes
Serves 4

1 pound extra-lean ground
　turkey breast
1 large egg
½ cup almond flour
　or whole wheat
　bread crumbs
2 scallions, chopped
2 tablespoons chopped
　fresh parsley
1 teaspoon minced garlic
¼ teaspoon freshly ground
　black pepper
2 teaspoons olive oil
3 cups All-Purpose
　Marinara Sauce
　(page 124) or
　store-bought
4 cups spiralized zucchini

1. In a medium bowl, mix together the turkey, egg, almond flour, scallions, parsley, garlic, and pepper until well combined. Using your hands, roll the mixture into 1-inch meatballs.

2. In a large skillet, heat the oil over medium-high heat. Add the meatballs and cook, turning occasionally, for about 15 minutes, or until browned and cooked through.

3. Meanwhile, in a medium saucepan, heat the marinara over medium heat for 10 minutes to heat through.

4. To serve, place the zucchini noodles in a large serving bowl. Arrange the meatballs over the noodles and pour the sauce over the top. Store the meatballs, sauce, and zucchini noodles in separate sealed containers in the refrigerator for up to 4 days.

Per serving: Calories: 373; Protein: 30g; Carbohydrates: 32g; Fiber: 9g; Total fat: 15g; Saturated fat: 2g; Sugar: 17g; Sodium: 168mg

Peanutty Pork-Topped Veggie Slaw ⚡

This dish uses sesame oil as a good-for-you oil option and includes lean ground pork to cut down on fat. The Avocado Yogurt Dressing (page 126) provides a rich creaminess, along with heart-healthy unsaturated fats and probiotics to promote heart and gut health.

GLUTEN-FREE

Prep time: 20 minutes
Cook time: 10 minutes
Serves 2

1 teaspoon sesame oil
8 ounces lean ground pork
¼ cup Thai-Inspired
   Peanut Sauce (page 125)
   or store-bought
3 cups shredded cabbage
2 cups shredded kale
1 large carrot, shredded
½ cup shredded radish
1 scallion, thinly sliced
¼ cup Avocado Yogurt
   Dressing (page 126) or
   store-bought

1. In a large skillet, heat the oil over medium-high heat. Add the pork and sauté for about 10 minutes, or until the meat is cooked through. Remove the skillet from the heat and stir in the peanut sauce.

2. Meanwhile, in a medium bowl, toss together the cabbage, kale, carrot, radish, scallion, and dressing until evenly combined.

3. Divide the slaw between two plates, top with the spicy pork mixture, and serve.

TIP: You can use this pork mixture as a topping for a tasty grain bowl.

Per serving: Calories: 403; Protein: 33g; Carbohydrates: 20g; Fiber: 7g; Total fat: 24g; Saturated fat: 4g; Sugar: 8.5g; Sodium: 296mg

Dijon Thyme Pork Tenderloin ⊛⚡

This dish has a lot going for it: In addition to the pork, you only need four pantry staples, and the dish is ready in a mere 30 minutes. Garlic adds flavor and inflammation-lowering properties, whereas thyme, honey, and Dijon mustard create wonderfully balanced sweet, spicy, and herbaceous notes.

ALLERGEN-FREE **GLUTEN-FREE**
DAIRY-FREE **NUT-FREE**

Prep time: 10 minutes
Cook time: 20 minutes
Serves 2

2 tablespoons
   Dijon mustard
1 tablespoon honey
½ teaspoon minced garlic
1 teaspoon dried thyme
10 ounces pork tenderloin
Sea salt
Freshly ground
   black pepper

1. Preheat the oven to 350°F.

2. In a small bowl, stir together the mustard, honey, garlic, and thyme until well combined.

3. Pat dry the pork with paper towels and season lightly with salt and pepper. Place the pork in a 9-inch square baking dish and spread it with the mustard mixture.

4. Bake for 20 minutes, or until the pork is no longer pink in the center.

5. Let the meat rest for 10 minutes before cutting into slices and serving.

TIP: Make sure you trim off any visible fat and the thin white membrane on this cut of meat before cooking it.

Per serving: Calories: 198; Protein: 27g; Carbohydrates: 9g; Fiber: 0g; Total fat: 3.5g; Saturated fat: 1g; Sugar: 8g; Sodium: 498mg

Ground Beef and Veggie Skillet ⬤

This skillet meal is high in iron and protein and packed with fiber and antioxidants that can protect against prostate cancer and improve skin and heart health. Zucchini and bell peppers provide excellent hydration because they're mostly made up of water.

ALLERGEN-FREE **GLUTEN-FREE**
DAIRY-FREE **NUT-FREE**

Prep time: 15 minutes
Cook time: 25 minutes
Serves 4

1 pound ground beef
  (93% lean)
1 sweet onion, chopped
12 white button
  mushrooms, quartered
2 teaspoons minced garlic
2 teaspoons Italian
  seasoning
2 zucchini, chopped
1 yellow bell
  pepper, chopped
1 cup halved cherry
  tomatoes
Sea salt
Freshly ground
  black pepper

1. In a large dry skillet, sauté the beef over medium-high heat for about 10 minutes, or until it is cooked through.

2. Add the onion, mushrooms, garlic, and Italian seasoning and sauté for about 8 minutes, or until softened.

3. Add the zucchini, bell pepper, and tomatoes and cook for about 7 minutes, or until the vegetables are softened.

4. Season lightly with salt and pepper and serve. Store leftovers in a sealed container in the refrigerator for up to 4 days.

TIP: If extra-lean ground beef is not available, you can use any other type, but make sure you drain off any fat in the skillet after it is cooked and before adding the other ingredients.

Per serving: Calories: 202; Protein: 27g; Carbohydrates: 15g; Fiber: 2.5g; Total fat: 4g; Saturated fat: 2g; Sugar: 9.5g; Sodium: 106mg

Sheet Pan Steak Fajitas ⚡

Inspired by the Tex-Mex classic, these fajitas are the perfect meal-prepping recipe because you can cook the ingredients in bulk on one sheet pan. You'll then have cooked meat and veggies ready for a variety of meals all week. This recipe is dairy-free, but you can add cheese, such as queso fresco or shredded Cheddar. If you're dialing back the carbs, substitute lettuce for the corn tortillas.

DAIRY-FREE **NUT-FREE**
GLUTEN-FREE

Prep time: 15 minutes
Cook time: 15 minutes
Serves 4

1 tablespoon fajita
    seasoning or Italian
    seasoning
1 teaspoon chili powder
12 ounces beef sirloin
    steak, cut against the
    grain into ¼-inch-
    thick slices
1 sweet onion, cut
    crosswise into
    ½-inch-thick slices
3 bell peppers (green
    and red), cut into
    ½-inch-wide strips
1 tablespoon olive oil
Freshly ground
    black pepper
4 (6-inch) corn tortillas

1. Position a rack in the top third of the oven and preheat the oven to broil. Line a sheet pan with aluminum foil.

2. In a small bowl, mix together the fajita seasoning and chili powder. Add the steak strips and toss until coated.

3. Arrange the steak on one-third of the prepared sheet pan and spread out the onion and bell peppers on the remaining two-thirds. Drizzle the veggies with the oil, season with pepper, and toss until coated.

4. Broil for 5 minutes. Stir the veggies and meat and continue to broil for another 5 to 7 minutes, until the meat is cooked but still slightly pink and the vegetables are tender.

5. Serve the fajita mixture wrapped in tortillas. Store leftover fajita mixture and tortillas in separate containers in the refrigerator for up to 4 days.

TIP: Top the fajitas with chopped tomato, sour cream, shredded cheese, hot peppers, or chopped avocado.

Per serving: Calories: 266; Protein: 21g; Carbohydrates: 22g; Fiber: 3.5g; Total fat: 10g; Saturated fat: 3g; Sugar: 6.5g; Sodium: 50mg

Beef Kebabs with Garlic Marinade

Feel free to vary the veggies in these kebabs by going with broccoli, cauliflower, carrots, squash, or zucchini. If you use wooden skewers, be sure to soak them in water for at least 30 minutes before putting them under the broiler.

ALLERGEN-FREE **GLUTEN-FREE**
DAIRY-FREE **NUT-FREE**

Prep time: 15 minutes, plus 2 hours to marinate and 30 minutes to come to room temperature
Cook time: 10 minutes
Serves 2

¼ cup olive oil
1 tablespoon apple cider vinegar
2 teaspoons minced garlic
1 tablespoon chopped fresh rosemary or 1 teaspoon dried
¼ teaspoon freshly ground black pepper
8 ounces beef sirloin or flat iron steak, cut into 8 equal chunks
8 medium white button mushrooms
8 Brussels sprouts, trimmed and halved
1 red onion, cut into 8 wedges
1 red bell pepper, cut into 8 pieces

1. In a medium bowl, stir together the oil, vinegar, garlic, rosemary, and pepper until well blended. Remove 2 tablespoons of the marinade and set it aside in a small bowl.

2. Add the beef chunks to the medium bowl with the marinade and toss until coated. Cover with plastic wrap and refrigerate for at least 2 hours.

3. When you're ready to cook, let the meat stand at room temperature for at least 30 minutes.

4. Position a rack in the top third of the oven and preheat the oven to broil. Line a baking sheet with aluminum foil.

5. Thread the beef chunks and vegetables onto four metal or wooden skewers, using two of each ingredient on each. Brush the vegetables with the reserved marinade.

6. Place the skewers on the prepared baking sheet and broil for 5 minutes. Turn the skewers and continue to broil for 4 to 6 minutes for medium.

7. Let the kebabs rest for 5 minutes before serving. To store leftovers, pull the cooked ingredients off the skewers and store in a sealed container in the refrigerator for up to 4 days.

Per serving: Calories: 422; Protein: 29g; Carbohydrates: 18g; Fiber: 5g; Total fat: 26g; Saturated fat: 5.5g; Sugar: 8g; Sodium: 79mg

Roasted Flank Steak with Root Vegetables ⊖

This recipe calls for meat and vegetables to be cooked on one sheet pan for simple cleanup. Lean flank steak is a good protein option. The roasted root veggies provide fiber, antioxidants, and complex carbs to keep you fuller longer.

ALLERGEN-FREE **GLUTEN-FREE**
DAIRY-FREE **NUT-FREE**

Prep time: 15 minutes
Cook time: 25 minutes
Serves 2

1 sweet potato,
    peeled and cut into
    1-inch chunks
2 carrots, cut into
    1-inch chunks
2 parsnips, peeled and cut
    into 1-inch chunks
½ sweet onion, cut into
    1-inch chunks
1 tablespoon olive oil
½ teaspoon ground cumin
8 ounces flank steak
Sea salt
Freshly ground
    black pepper

1. Preheat the oven to 400°F. Line a sheet pan with aluminum foil.

2. Spread the sweet potato, carrots, parsnips, and onion on two-thirds of the prepared sheet pan. Drizzle with the oil, sprinkle with the cumin, and toss until coated.

3. Roast for 12 minutes, remove from the oven, and turn the vegetables. Add the steak to the empty part of the sheet pan and roast with the vegetables for 6 minutes. Flip the steak and continue to roast for another 6 minutes, or until the vegetables are tender and the steak is cooked to medium.

4. Let the meat rest for 10 minutes. Cut the steak thinly against the grain and serve with the vegetables.

TIP: Skirt steak is a good choice if flank steak is unavailable. Trim off any visible fat before roasting; to serve, cut it into very thin slices to ensure that the meat is tender.

Per serving: Calories: 471; Protein: 30g; Carbohydrates: 56g; Fiber: 13g; Total fat: 15g; Saturated fat: 4g; Sugar: 18g; Sodium: 230mg

Beef Stir-Fry ⊖

Stir-fries are easy to cook, and you can make a large batch for meals throughout the week. This recipe is packed with vitamin- and mineral-rich veggies representing the entire spectrum of the rainbow. Anti-inflammatory ginger adds a kick.

DAIRY-FREE **GLUTEN-FREE**

Prep time: 15 minutes
Cook time: 20 minutes
Serves 2

1 tablespoon sesame oil
8 ounces beef sirloin steak, cut against the grain into ¼-inch-thick slices
1 large carrot, thinly sliced
1 red bell pepper, cut into ¼-inch-wide strips
10 white button mushrooms, thinly sliced
2 teaspoons minced garlic
1 teaspoon grated peeled fresh ginger
2 cups small broccoli florets
1 cup (1-inch pieces) green beans
2 teaspoons coconut aminos
2 scallions, green part only, thinly sliced

1. In a large skillet, heat the oil over medium-high heat. Add the beef and sauté for about 7 minutes, or until just cooked through. Using a slotted spoon, transfer the beef to a plate and set aside.

2. Add the carrot, bell pepper, mushrooms, garlic, and ginger to the skillet and sauté for about 8 minutes, or until tender-crisp.

3. Add the broccoli, green beans, and coconut aminos and sauté for about 5 minutes, or until tender-crisp.

4. Return the beef to the skillet, toss until combined, and serve with a sprinkling of scallions. Store leftovers in a sealed container in the refrigerator for up to 4 days.

TIP: Try this dish over brown rice or even over a bed of shredded lettuce or bean sprouts. You can use sliced chicken in place of the beef if you prefer.

Per serving: Calories: 296; Protein: 32g; Carbohydrates: 18g; Fiber: 5.5g; Total fat: 12g; Saturated fat: 2.5g; Sugar: 9.5g; Sodium: 216mg

Blueberry Yogurt Granola Pops, page 116

Chapter Eight

DESSERTS

Berry Quinoa Pudding ⬭⚡

This fruity quinoa pudding contains fiber and antioxidants to improve your health while satisfying your sweet tooth. The topping of walnuts provides omega-3 fats found to improve cognition and supply fiber. But feel free to make your own fruit and nut picks.

DAIRY-FREE **VEGAN**
GLUTEN-FREE

Prep time: 10 minutes
Cook time: 20 minutes
Serves 4

1 cup unsweetened
   nondairy milk
1 cup water
¾ cup quinoa, rinsed
¼ cup gluten-free
   rolled oats
2 teaspoons pure
   vanilla extract
½ teaspoon ground
   cinnamon
Pinch sea salt
1 cup mixed fresh berries
¼ cup maple syrup
¼ cup chopped walnuts
   or unsweetened
   shredded coconut

1. In a medium saucepan, combine the milk, water, quinoa, oats, vanilla, cinnamon, and salt. Bring to a boil over medium-high heat, then reduce the heat to low, partially cover, and simmer, stirring occasionally, for about 20 minutes, or until the quinoa is tender and the pudding is thick and creamy.

2. Serve topped with the fresh berries, a drizzle of maple syrup, and walnuts. Store leftovers in a sealed container in the refrigerator for up to 4 days.

TIP: Quinoa needs to be rinsed to remove a bitter coating called saponins, which can upset some people's stomachs. Some quinoa comes already rinsed, but if in doubt, don't skip this step.

Per serving: Calories: 261; Protein: 7g; Carbohydrates: 42g; Fiber: 4.5g; Total fat: 8g; Saturated fat: 0.5g; Sugar: 16g; Sodium: 123mg

Banana Bread Blondies

Banana bread has always been a comforting treat. This recipe combines classic banana bread flavors in a blondie spiced with cinnamon, vanilla, and nutmeg. Make sure to use very ripe bananas to achieve the appropriate texture and moistness.

DAIRY-FREE **VEGETARIAN**
GLUTEN-FREE

Prep time: 15 minutes
Cook time: 25 minutes
Makes 16 squares

Olive oil spray
1½ cups gluten-free
   oat flour
¾ cup almond flour
1 teaspoon baking soda
½ teaspoon ground
   cinnamon
¼ teaspoon
   ground nutmeg
⅛ teaspoon sea salt
3 ripe medium
   bananas, mashed
1 large egg
¼ cup natural
   almond butter
¼ cup maple syrup
1 teaspoon pure
   vanilla extract

1. Preheat the oven to 350°F. Lightly mist a 9-inch square baking dish with olive oil spray and set aside.

2. In a large bowl, mix together the oat flour, almond flour, baking soda, cinnamon, nutmeg, and salt.

3. In a medium bowl, whisk together the mashed bananas, egg, almond butter, maple syrup, and vanilla until blended. Add the wet ingredients to the dry ingredients and stir until just combined.

4. Pour the batter into the prepared pan, spreading it out evenly with a spatula.

5. Bake for 22 to 25 minutes until a toothpick inserted in the center comes out clean.

6. Let cool on a wire rack for 15 minutes. Cut into 16 squares and serve. Store the blondies in a sealed container in the refrigerator for up to 1 week or in the freezer for 1 month.

TIP: You can fold dark chocolate chips into the batter or drizzle melted chocolate or peanut butter over the top of the baked blondies if you want to get extra indulgent.

Per serving (2 squares): Calories: 243; Protein: 6g; Carbohydrates: 30g; Fiber: 4g; Total fat: 13g; Saturated fat: 1g; Sugar: 12g; Sodium: 59mg

Dark Chocolate Avocado Mousse

That's right, you can use fiber-packed, heart-healthy avocado in a dessert. It tastes great with chocolate and adds a silky-smooth consistency to this dairy-free mousse (you can go with your favorite plant-based milk). Maple syrup adds sweetness.

ALLERGEN-FREE **NUT-FREE**
DAIRY-FREE **VEGAN**
GLUTEN-FREE

Prep time: 10 minutes, plus 1 hour to chill
Serves 4

2 very ripe avocados, halved and pitted
⅓ cup Dutch process cocoa powder
¼ cup maple syrup
3 tablespoons unsweetened nondairy milk
1 teaspoon pure vanilla extract
Pinch sea salt

1. Scoop the avocado into a food processor or high-powered blender. Add the cocoa powder, maple syrup, milk, vanilla, and salt and blend for about 2 minutes, or until very smooth and creamy, scraping down the sides as needed.

2. Dividing evenly, spoon the mousse into four bowls and refrigerate for at least 1 hour to chill.

3. Store leftovers in a sealed container in the refrigerator for up to 3 days.

TIP: This mousse is fabulous with whipped coconut cream. Refrigerate a 14-ounce can of coconut milk overnight, then open it carefully and spoon the hardened layer at the top into a medium bowl. Add 1 teaspoon vanilla and beat with an electric mixer until fluffy. Refrigerate any leftovers in a sealed container for up to 1 week.

Per serving: Calories: 181; Protein: 3g; Carbohydrates: 23g; Fiber: 7g; Total fat: 11g; Saturated fat: 1.5g; Sugar: 12g; Sodium: 89mg

Vanilla N'ice Cream ✽

Who doesn't love ice cream on a warm day or served with a slice of pie? This lightened-up version uses bananas and nondairy milk for the base—you can't get any cleaner than that! It's healthy, simple to make, and sweetened only with the bananas and a little vanilla. Add other ingredients like berries, nut butter, or unsweetened shredded coconut to change the flavor.

ALLERGEN-FREE   **NUT-FREE**
DAIRY-FREE   **VEGAN**
GLUTEN-FREE

Prep time: 10 minutes, plus 2 hours to freeze
Serves 2

2 large bananas, sliced and frozen

2 to 4 tablespoons unsweetened nondairy milk

2 teaspoons pure vanilla extract

1.   Line a 9-by-5-inch loaf pan with parchment paper.

2.   In a food processor or high-powered blender, combine the frozen banana slices, 2 tablespoons of milk, and the vanilla and blend on high speed, scraping down the sides with a spatula at least once, until the mixture resembles soft-serve ice cream. If the mixture is too thick or not blended well, add the remaining 2 tablespoons of milk and continue to blend.

3.   Transfer the mixture to the preapred loaf pan and freeze until it scoops like regular ice cream, about 2 hours.

4.   Serve immediately. Store leftovers in a sealed container in the freezer. When you want to serve it, let sit at room temperature for 30 minutes so it will be scoopable.

TIP: For a tempting peanut butter n'ice cream, add ¼ cup natural peanut butter to the blender with the other ingredients.

Per serving: Calories: 88; Protein: 1g; Carbohydrates: 19g; Fiber: 2g; Total fat: 0.5g; Saturated fat: 0g; Sugar: 0g; Sodium: 24mg

Chocolate-Drizzled Almond Rice Squares ✷

These chocolate-topped rice treats are sweetened with maple syrup. The almond butter provides some filling fat, protein, and fiber, so you won't feel tempted to reach for a second one—although it's understandable if you do! The higher the cacao content, the higher the level of antioxidants. Look for chocolate with a cacao content of at least 70 percent.

DAIRY-FREE **VEGAN**
GLUTEN-FREE

Prep time: 15 minutes, plus 2 hours to chill
Makes 16 squares

½ cup natural almond butter, at room temperature
¼ cup maple syrup
1 teaspoon pure vanilla extract
Pinch sea salt
6 cups puffed rice cereal
¾ cup dairy-free dark chocolate chips

1. Line an 8-inch square glass baking dish with parchment paper.

2. In a large bowl, mix together the almond butter, maple syrup, vanilla, and salt until very smooth. Add the rice cereal and stir until combined. Firmly press the mixture into the prepared baking dish and refrigerate for about 2 hours, or until firm.

3. Place the chocolate in a microwave-safe bowl and microwave in 30-second intervals, stirring after each interval, until it's melted and smooth.

4. Using the tines of a fork, drizzle the chocolate over the top of the squares. Let sit for a few minutes until the chocolate is set.

5. Cut into 2-inch squares and serve. Store leftovers in a sealed container in the refrigerator for up to 1 week.

TIP: Stir in 1 heaping tablespoon unsweetened cocoa powder with the almond butter and other ingredients to create a double-chocolate square.

Per serving (2 squares): Calories: 276; Protein: 6g; Carbohydrates: 32g; Fiber: 5.5g; Total fat: 18g; Saturated fat: 6.5g; Sugar: 15g; Sodium: 57mg

Strawberry Crumble Cups

Baked fruit desserts like crumbles are usually high in refined sugar and simple carbs. This clean version substitutes almonds and oats for white flour and applesauce and maple syrup for white sugar, considerably increasing the dessert's healthy fat and fiber content. As a bonus, the dessert is baked in a muffin pan for perfect individual portions.

DAIRY-FREE **VEGAN**
GLUTEN-FREE

Prep time: 15 minutes, plus time to chill
Cook time: 30 minutes
Makes 12 crumble cups

For the filling
3 cups sliced strawberries
3 tablespoons arrowroot
1 tablespoon fresh
  lemon juice

For the crust
1 cup gluten-free
  rolled oats
1 cup gluten-free oat flour
1 cup almond flour
¼ teaspoon
  ground nutmeg
¼ teaspoon sea salt
¼ cup unsweetened
  applesauce, plus more
  as needed
¼ cup coconut oil, at room
  temperature
¼ cup maple syrup

1. Preheat the oven to 350°F. Line 12 cups of a muffin tin with foil-lined muffin cups.

To make the filling

2. In a medium saucepan, combine the strawberries, arrowroot, and lemon juice. Bring to a simmer over medium-high heat, stirring constantly, and cook for about 4 minutes, or until the filling is thick. Remove the saucepan from the heat and set aside.

To make the crust

3. In a large bowl, mix together the oats, oat flour, almond flour, nutmeg, and salt. Add the applesauce, coconut oil, and maple syrup and mix until the mixture resembles coarse crumbs and holds together when pressed. Add more applesauce if needed to reach the right consistency.

4. Measure out one-quarter of the crust mixture to use as the crumble topping and set aside in a small bowl. Divide the remaining mixture equally among the 12 muffin cups, pressing it firmly into the bottoms and up the sides to create a cup shape.

$\longrightarrow$

5. Spoon the strawberry filling into the cups to come about ⅛ inch from the top of the foil cups. Crumble the reserved crust mixture over the strawberry filling.

6. Bake for 25 to 30 minutes until the crust is firm and golden brown and the filling is bubbling.

7. Let cool completely in the pan on a wire rack. Transfer to a sealed container and refrigerate until well chilled, then serve.

8. Store leftovers in a sealed container in the refrigerator for up to 5 days or in the freezer for up to 1 month.

TIP: Try using any berries, or sliced apples or pears, instead of strawberries. Make sure you cook down the fruit filling to remove as much liquid as possible or the crumbles will be too moist to hold together.

Per serving (1 crumble cup): Calories: 181; Protein: 4g; Carbohydrates: 20g; Fiber: 3g; Total fat: 9.5g; Saturated fat: 4.5g; Sugar: 7g; Sodium: 51mg

Lemon Almond Bars

These lemon bars have a crust naturally sweetened with Medjool dates.

Prep time: 15 minutes, plus 6 hours to chill
Cook time: 35 minutes
Makes 16 bars

For the crust
1 cup almond flour
3 pitted Medjool dates
¼ cup coconut oil
Pinch sea salt

For the filling
5 large eggs
Grated zest of 1 lemon
½ cup fresh lemon juice
   (3 or 4 lemons)
⅓ cup maple syrup
1 teaspoon pure
   vanilla extract
⅛ teaspoon sea salt
3 tablespoons arrowroot
   or cornstarch

To make the crust

1. Preheat the oven to 350°F. Line an 8-inch square baking dish with parchment paper.

2. In a blender, combine the almond flour, dates, coconut oil, and salt and pulse until the mixture is crumbly and holds together when pressed.

3. Press the almond mixture evenly into the prepared baking dish and bake for 10 minutes, or until lightly golden brown.

4. Transfer the crust to a wire rack to cool completely. Leave the oven on.

To make the filling

5. In a medium bowl, whisk together the eggs, lemon zest, lemon juice, maple syrup, vanilla, and salt. Add the arrowroot and whisk until fully blended.

6. Pour the lemon mixture over the cooled crust, transfer to the oven, and bake for 25 minutes, or until the topping is just set.

7. Let the bars cool completely on a wire rack. Cover with plastic wrap and refrigerate for at least 6 hours.

8. Cut the bars into 16 squares and serve. Store in a sealed container in the refrigerator for up to 1 week.

Per serving (1 bar): Calories: 122; Protein: 3g; Carbohydrates: 10g; Fiber: 1g; Total fat: 8g; Saturated fat: 3.5g; Sugar: 6.5g; Sodium: 42mg

Blueberry Yogurt Granola Pops ⚙

The best thing about this yogurt pop, aside from its flavor, is that it can double as a snack or breakfast on the go. Greek yogurt has protein to fill you up as well as probiotics to support gut health. The blueberries offer both fiber and natural sweetness. The granola adds an unexpected crunch.

GLUTEN-FREE | **VEGETARIAN**

Prep time: 10 minutes, plus 6 hours to chill
Makes 6 pops

2 cups blueberries
2 cups 0% plain
  Greek yogurt
2 tablespoons honey
¼ teaspoon ground
  cinnamon
6 tablespoons gluten-free
  granola, large pieces
  crushed

1. Have ready six 3-ounce ice pop molds.

2. In a blender, puree the blueberries on high speed.

3. In a medium bowl, whisk together the yogurt, honey, and cinnamon. Add the blueberry puree and swirl it into the yogurt mixture, leaving streaks.

4. Place 1 tablespoon of granola into each pop mold and carefully pour the yogurt mixture into each mold. Insert the pop sticks into each pop, cover, and freeze for about 6 hours, until very firm.

TIP: Run hot water on the outside of the mold for 10 seconds to easily release the pop.

Per serving (1 pop): Calories: 124; Protein: 9g; Carbohydrates: 21g; Fiber: 1.5g; Total fat: 1g; Saturated fat: 0g; Sugar: 15g; Sodium: 47mg

Pico de Gallo, page 121

Chapter Nine

HOMEMADE STAPLES

Low-Sodium Vegetable Broth ⊙

A basic vegetable broth can pack a mighty flavor punch. This fragrant vegan broth has inflammation-lowering properties from garlic and is low in sodium to keep your heart healthy and help you beat bloat.

ALLERGEN-FREE **NUT-FREE**
DAIRY-FREE **VEGAN**
GLUTEN-FREE

Prep time: 10 minutes
Cook time: 3 hours
Makes 8 cups

2 small sweet onions, roughly chopped

2 large carrots, roughly chopped

5 celery stalks with leafy tops, roughly chopped

6 garlic cloves, peeled and smashed

4 parsley sprigs

3 thyme sprigs

3 bay leaves

1 teaspoon black peppercorns

10 cups water

1. In a large stockpot, combine the onions, carrots, celery, garlic, parsley, thyme, bay leaves, peppercorns, and water. Cover and bring to a boil over high heat. Reduce the heat to low and simmer, stirring occasionally, for 3 hours.

2. Strain the broth through a fine-mesh sieve into a heatproof bowl or pitcher and discard the solids.

3. Use immediately or let cool, transfer to sealed containers or mason jars, and store in the refrigerator for up to 5 days or in the freezer for up to 1 month.

TIP: To make beef broth, add 2 pounds of beef bones to the basic vegetable broth recipe and simmer for 6 to 7 hours. For chicken broth, add 2 chicken carcasses to the basic vegetable broth recipe and simmer for 4 to 5 hours.

Per serving (1 cup): Calories: 11; Protein: 0g; Carbohydrates: 2g; Fiber: 0g; Total fat: 0g; Saturated fat: 0g; Sugar: 1.5g; Sodium: 42mg

Pico de Gallo

Pico de gallo is the perfect companion for fish tacos, egg or tofu scrambles, salads, and kebabs. The lycopene-containing tomatoes will improve your heart and skin health as well as boost your hydration.

ALLERGEN-FREE **NUT-FREE**
DAIRY-FREE **VEGAN**
GLUTEN-FREE

Prep time: 20 minutes
Makes 2 cups

3 large tomatoes, seeded
   and chopped
½ sweet onion, chopped
1 jalapeño pepper, seeded
   and chopped
¼ cup chopped fresh
   cilantro
2 tablespoons chopped
   fresh parsley
Grated zest of 1 lime
Juice of 1 lime
Sea salt
Freshly ground
   black pepper

In a medium bowl, mix together the tomatoes, onion, jalapeño, cilantro, parsley, lime zest, and lime juice. Season lightly with salt and pepper and serve immediately. Store leftovers in a sealed container in the refrigerator for up to 5 days.

TIP: If you like a little heat in your salsa, leave the seeds in the jalapeño or use a hotter chile such as serrano or habanero.

Per serving (½ cup): Calories: 42; Protein: 2g; Carbohydrates: 10g; Fiber: 2.5g; Total fat: 0.5g; Saturated fat: 0g; Sugar: 6g; Sodium: 48mg

Citrus Thyme Dressing

Orange zest, lemon zest, and thyme come together for a citrusy herbal dressing that works well on meat, poultry, fish, and leafy greens. Apple cider vinegar adds an acidic bite, and its consumption may correlate with improved gut health and digestion.

ALLERGEN-FREE	NUT-FREE
DAIRY-FREE	VEGAN
GLUTEN-FREE	

Prep time: 5 minutes
Makes about ¾ cup

½ cup extra-virgin olive oil

2 tablespoons apple cider vinegar

Grated zest of 1 lemon

Juice of 1 lemon

1 teaspoon grated orange zest

1 teaspoon chopped fresh thyme

Sea salt

Freshly ground black pepper

In a small bowl, whisk together the oil, vinegar, lemon zest, lemon juice, orange zest, and thyme until well blended. Season lightly with salt and pepper. Use immediately or store in a sealed container in the refrigerator for up to 2 weeks. Shake well before serving.

TIP: This is a base dressing that can be jazzed up with chopped pureed fruit or flavored vinegar to create different flavor profiles. Or swap in a different herb.

Per serving (2 tablespoons): Calories: 162; Protein: 0g; Carbohydrates: 1g; Fiber: 0g; Total fat: 18g; Saturated fat: 2.5g; Sugar: 0.5g; Sodium: 27mg

Tzatziki Sauce ⊛◉⚡

Tzatziki is a yogurt-based sauce that's rich and creamy with a refreshing finish, thanks to English cucumber and fresh dill. Although low in calories and fat, this sauce evokes the decadence of far-less-healthy blue cheese and Caesar dressings, giving you the texture you crave in a clean eating recipe.

GLUTEN-FREE **VEGETARIAN**
NUT-FREE

Prep time: 15 minutes
Makes 2 cups

1 cup 0% plain
  Greek yogurt
1 large English cucumber,
  coarsely grated and
  liquid squeezed out
Grated zest of 1 lemon
Juice of 1 lemon
2 tablespoons chopped
  fresh dill
1 teaspoon minced garlic
Sea salt
Freshly ground
  black pepper

In a medium bowl, mix together the yogurt, cucumber, lemon zest, lemon juice, dill, and garlic. Season lightly with salt and pepper and serve immediately or store in a sealed container in the refrigerator for up to 4 days.

TIP: Feel free to serve this sauce as a condiment for sandwiches or a dressing for salads. It makes a great dip, paired with whole-grain pita chips or vegetable crudités. If desired, you can add chopped walnuts or pistachios for a bit of crunch.

Per serving (¼ cup): Calories: 24; Protein: 3g; Carbohydrates: 2g; Fiber: 0g; Total fat: 0g; Saturated fat: 0g; Sugar: 1.5g; Sodium: 31mg

All-Purpose Marinara Sauce ⊖

Marinara is a classic red tomato sauce that can brighten up a plate of whole wheat pasta or zoodles. It even tastes great when you scoop it up with a piece of whole wheat baguette. Try sprinkling additional red pepper flakes on it after the sauce is plated.

Prep time: 15 minutes
Cook time: 30 minutes
Makes 3 cups

2 teaspoons olive oil
1 sweet onion, chopped
1 red bell pepper, chopped
1 tablespoon minced garlic
1 (28-ounce) can no-salt-
    added diced tomatoes
¼ cup chopped fresh basil
    or 2 tablespoons dried
2 tablespoons chopped
    fresh oregano or
    1 tablespoon dried
Pinch red pepper flakes
Sea salt
Freshly ground
    black pepper

1. In a large saucepan, heat the oil over medium-high heat. Add the onion, bell pepper, and garlic and sauté for about 5 minutes, or until softened.

2. Stir in the tomatoes with their juices, basil, oregano, and red pepper flakes. Bring the sauce to a high simmer, then reduce the heat to low and simmer for 25 minutes to mellow the flavors.

3. Season lightly with salt and black pepper and serve immediately. Store leftovers in a sealed container in the refrigerator for up to 5 days or in the freezer for up to 3 months.

TIP: Add ½ cup chopped sun-dried tomatoes to the sauce to add a depth of tomato flavor. If using oil-marinated sun-dried tomatoes, rinse them well in warm water and pat dry before using.

Per serving (¾ cup): Calories: 111; Protein: 3g; Carbohydrates: 19g; Fiber: 4.5g; Total fat: 2.5g; Saturated fat: 0.5g; Sugar: 10g; Sodium: 72mg

Thai-Inspired Peanut Sauce ⊙⚡

This silky-smooth peanut sauce is perfect for Thai-inspired lettuce wraps, chicken or steak kebabs, grilled salmon, and more. If you like your peanut sauce on the spicy side, go heavier on the sambal, or dial it back for a milder flavor. Ginger aids in nausea relief and indigestion prevention, and it has anti-inflammatory properties that can improve your overall health.

DAIRY-FREE　**VEGAN**
GLUTEN-FREE

Prep time: 10 minutes
Makes about ¾ cup

½ cup natural
　peanut butter
2 tablespoons
　coconut aminos
Juice of ½ lime
2 teaspoons minced garlic
2 teaspoons sambal oelek
　or other chile paste
1 teaspoon grated peeled
　fresh ginger
1 teaspoon sesame oil
1 to 2 tablespoons water
　(optional)

In a blender, combine the peanut butter, coconut aminos, lime juice, garlic, sambal, ginger, and sesame oil and puree until smooth. If needed, add water, 1 teaspoon at a time, until the sauce reaches the desired consistency. Use immediately or store in a sealed container in the refrigerator for up to 2 weeks.

TIP: Any nut or seed butter will work for this recipe.

Per serving (2 tablespoons): Calories: 142; Protein: 5g; Carbohydrates: 6g; Fiber: 1.5g; Total fat: 12g; Saturated fat: 2g; Sugar: 2g; Sodium: 117mg

Avocado Yogurt Dressing ⬭⚡

Avocado and Greek yogurt are a dynamic duo for heart and gut health. Aside from being refreshing, the combination adds depth to salads and grain bowls. Lemon juice and zest brighten, and black pepper adds a hint of spice. Use this dressing on salads, as a marinade for chicken or fish, or as a dip for freshly sliced veggies.

GLUTEN-FREE **VEGETARIAN** **NUT-FREE**

Prep time: 10 minutes
Makes about 1½ cups

1 avocado, halved
   and pitted
⅓ cup 0% plain
   Greek yogurt
2 tablespoons extra-virgin
   olive oil
Grated zest of ½ lemon
Juice of ½ lemon
2 tablespoons chopped
   fresh parsley
1 teaspoon minced garlic
¼ teaspoon sea salt
Freshly ground
   black pepper
1 to 2 tablespoons water
   (optional)

Scoop the avocado into a blender. Add the yogurt, oil, lemon zest, lemon juice, parsley, garlic, salt, and pepper to taste and puree, scraping down the sides once, until smooth. If needed, add water, 1 teaspoon at a time, until the dressing reaches the desired consistency. Use immediately or store in a sealed container in the refrigerator for up to 2 weeks.

TIP: This dressing works well with a drizzle of Sriracha or hot sauce, especially in salads or falafel pita sandwiches. The heat, combined with the cooling qualities of avocado and yogurt, creates a well-rounded balance of flavor. Try it!

Per serving (¼ cup): Calories: 90; Protein: 2g; Carbohydrates: 4g; Fiber: 1.5g; Total fat: 8g; Saturated fat: 1g; Sugar: 1g; Sodium: 105mg

Classic Basil Pesto ⊛⊜⊘

Pesto is a light herbaceous sauce that complements pasta, whole-grain bread, meats, and fish. This classic version is made with fresh basil. Parmigiano-Reggiano cheese and pine nuts round out the flavors and add richness and texture.

GLUTEN-FREE   **VEGETARIAN**

Prep time: 10 minutes
Makes about 1 cup

2 cups fresh basil leaves
¼ cup pine nuts
¼ cup grated Parmigiano-
   Reggiano cheese
1 tablespoon minced garlic
½ cup extra-virgin olive oil
Sea salt
Freshly ground
   black pepper

1. In a blender, combine the basil, pine nuts, Parmigiano-Reggiano, and garlic and pulse until finely chopped.

2. While the blender is running, pour in the oil in a thin stream and puree until the pesto is thick. Season lightly with salt and pepper.

3. Use immediately or store in a sealed container in the refrigerator for up to 2 weeks.

TIP: Any herb or dark leafy green (or a combination of several) can be used in pesto in the same amount as the basil.

Per serving (1 tablespoon): Calories: 81; Protein: 1g; Carbohydrates: 1g; Fiber: 0g; Total fat: 8.5g; Saturated fat: 1g; Sugar: 0g; Sodium: 33mg

MEASUREMENT CONVERSIONS

VOLUME EQUIVALENTS	U.S. STANDARD	U.S. STANDARD (OUNCES)	METRIC (APPROXIMATE)
LIQUID	2 tablespoons	1 fl. oz.	30 mL
	¼ cup	2 fl. oz.	60 mL
	½ cup	4 fl. oz.	120 mL
	1 cup	8 fl. oz.	240 mL
	1½ cups	12 fl. oz.	355 mL
	2 cups or 1 pint	16 fl. oz.	475 mL
	4 cups or 1 quart	32 fl. oz.	1 L
	1 gallon	128 fl. oz.	4 L
DRY	⅛ teaspoon	—	0.5 mL
	¼ teaspoon	—	1 mL
	½ teaspoon	—	2 mL
	¾ teaspoon	—	4 mL
	1 teaspoon	—	5 mL
	1 tablespoon	—	15 mL
	¼ cup	—	59 mL
	⅓ cup	—	79 mL
	½ cup	—	118 mL
	⅔ cup	—	156 mL
	¾ cup	—	177 mL
	1 cup	—	235 mL
	2 cups or 1 pint	—	475 mL
	3 cups	—	700 mL
	4 cups or 1 quart	—	1 L
	½ gallon	—	2 L
	1 gallon	—	4 L

OVEN TEMPERATURES

FAHRENHEIT	CELSIUS (APPROXIMATE)
250°F	120°C
300°F	150°C
325°F	165°C
350°F	180°C
375°F	190°C
400°F	200°C
425°F	220°C
450°F	230°C

WEIGHT EQUIVALENTS

U.S. STANDARD	METRIC (APPROXIMATE)
½ ounce	15 g
1 ounce	30 g
2 ounces	60 g
4 ounces	115 g
8 ounces	225 g
12 ounces	340 g
16 ounces or 1 pound	455 g

RESOURCES

If you are looking to learn more about a clean eating approach to food, you can always browse Callisto Media's wide selection of cookbooks and introductory guides to vegan, vegetarian, paleo, ketogenic, Mediterranean, and other diet-focused lifestyles.

You can learn more about best fish and seafood practices by searching SeafoodWatch .org, where you can get the best recommendations for sustainable purchases locally.

You can browse reputable sources, like Healthline (Healthline.com), to read up on the health benefits of certain clean eating superfoods. Healthline links to various studies.

Please feel free to reach out to me, Isadora, if you're interested in more personalized coaching to help you continue your clean eating journey. You can reach me by email, isadora@isadorabaum.com, on Instagram by my handle @izeating, or through my website: IsadoraBaum.com.

INDEX

Acknowledgments

I would like to thank my collaborators in producing *Clean Eating for Beginners* and the wonderful team at Callisto Media. I would also like to give thanks to the various mentors and editors with whom I have worked over the years who have helped shape my career through new experiences and ventures. Last, and most important, I'd like to thank my mother, for she is my rock. I would never be where and who I am today without her unconditional love and support.

About the Author

 **Isadora Baum** is a freelance writer, certified health coach, and author. She graduated from Northwestern University and has written for various websites and publications, including *Men's Health*, *Women's Health*, Livestrong, Well + Good, *Allure*, Bustle, *Self*, Eat This, Not That!, *Health*, and Allrecipes.com.

She is the author of *5-Minute Energy* as well as *Self-Love Games & Activities: 125 Word Searches, Mazes, & Games to Boost Your Happiness, Resilience, & Well-Being*. She loves a great margarita, a new adventure, the chance to sing and dance, a HIIT or boxing workout, a scoop of peanut butter, and always, a reason to laugh.

CPSIA information can be obtained
at www.ICGtesting.com
Printed in the USA
JSHW051013220821
18053JS00003B/11